THE PROCESS PERSPECTIVE II

THE PROCESS PERSPECTIVE II

By John B. Cobb, Jr.

Edited by Jeanyne B. Slettom

CHALICE
PRESS

ST. LOUIS, MISSOURI

Cover art: © Getty Images

Cover and interior design: Elizabeth Wright

Visit Chalice Press on the World Wide Web at
www.chalicepress.com

10 9 8 7 6 5 4 3 2 1   11 12 13 14 15 16

PRINT: 978-08272-29952   EPUB: 978-08272-30200
EPDF: 978-08272-30217

**Cataloging–in–Publication Data is available
from the Library of Congress**

Printed in United States of America

Contents

PART THREE: Faith

Acknowledgments

The chapters in the book are taken from short papers written for monthly publication on the Process & Faith Web site (http://www .processandfaith.org) in response to questions about process theology. In writing them, I made no effort to avoid repetition or to relate answers to one another in a coherent fashion. I am amazed by the skill with which Jeanyne Slettom has abridged and organized the material. May such repetitions as remain prove helpful to readers in that some main features of process theology that may seem initially strange will come to be clear and credible. Although the content is mine, the book is her achievement. I congratulate her for it.

John B. Cobb, Jr.

Introduction

I first met John B. Cobb, Jr., in the late 1990s—in northern Minnesota, of all places—on the shores of Rainy Lake, near the Canadian border. He had come to conduct a weeklong seminar on process theology for area clergy, and I was delighted to meet this man whose work I had read and admired for years.

What I discovered—as will you, as you read these pages—is that he is a gracious scholar with a genuine interest in understanding a student's question and answering it as helpfully as he can. He speaks with a slight Southern accent—just enough to convey a genteel calm—and he forms his thoughts so quickly that he also speaks in whole sentences, actually whole paragraphs, without any awkward pauses. I don't think I've ever heard him say "um."

Every morning he would arrive at the seminar setting with a half-page of paper on which he had jotted three or four points. From this he would proceed to talk for the next three hours, pausing to answer questions as they arose.

I start with this story because when I claim that reading this book will be like sitting in a seminar with John yourself, I want you to believe me. He really does talk like that. These answers were written out, but the tone is conversational, and the content is very much like what you would hear if you were sitting in a classroom with him. Reading this book you will experience his faith, his urgent concern for the world, and his understanding of God. He will gently show you the limits of what he is willing to believe, while allowing you the freedom to explore your own position.

The questions posed and answers given herein are all drawn from the Process & Faith Web site (http://www.processandfaith.org), where, since 1999, people have been asking, and John has been answering, questions related to process-relational theology. The questions and answers are featured each month on the "Ask Dr. Cobb" page. They appear here with some modifications—mostly to simplify the questions and to avoid unnecessary repetition.

In 2003, Chalice Press published *The Process Perspective: Frequently Asked Questions about Process Theology,* a collection of these questions and answers. Because of the book's popularity, and because new questions have been appearing every month since then, we have compiled a new collection culled from the site. The book is divided into three parts: metaphysics, science, and faith. Each section includes issues ranging from the timeless to the topical, and they can be read in order or wherever your mood takes you.

What they share in common is the presupposition of a process-relational world. In other words, they assume that God and the world are interrelated, interdependent, and dynamically interconnected. This is a God who is present in the world and affected by all that happens in it. This is a world that is also present in God, received into God's own being. Process-relational theology is a theology of transformation, of embodiment, and of hope. Perhaps its most transformative move is from a theology of divine omnipotence to divine omnipresence.

When God is present throughout creation and the whole of creation is included in the divine life (this is panentheism; if God were identical with creation it would be called pantheism), then the fate of the Earth becomes a crucial concern. What makes for a faithful response to social and economic issues takes on greater importance.

This pattern—of understanding how God works in the world, which then informs one's understanding of critical socioeconomic issues, which then provokes a deeper desire to live faithfully in a God-infused world—is roughly the one followed in this book.

We start with metaphysics because it is the branch of philosophy that deals with the nature of reality. Metaphysics differs from the natural sciences in that it deals with questions that are outside of scientific observation. It asks questions about the nature of being and how we know what we know. Metaphysics is a conceptual framework that we take with us everywhere we go, though we are largely unaware of it. It is the water in which we swim, and as has been observed, what's water to a fish?

Metaphysics has taken something of a drubbing from scientists and analytic philosophers, but even they, of course, have a conceptual framework that they bring to their work and the world. Thus the book begins with a very basic request for a simple description of process theology. Process theology is a conceptual framework, a way of viewing God and the world—in short, a metaphysic. This then leads to questions worthy of serious consideration: Should Christians even care about metaphysics? What difference does it make to the life of faith? Well, what happens when you have an inadequate or outdated metaphysic? You have the so-called new atheists, which the next question addresses.

The rest of Part One considers the nature of both human beings and God and the ways that God is present to us. It also shows the Whiteheadian trajectory of process theology, the one to which Dr. Cobb belongs. Alfred North Whitehead (1861–1947), the mathematician-turned-philosopher, represents the best-known, but by no means only, branch of process thought. Dr. Cobb is the preeminent theologian of this "school," so it is with some vigor that he responds, forty years after process theology burst upon the scene, to the concern that process theology may have "backed the wrong horse" in the theological sweepstakes of current seminary training.

If Part One explores the nature of God and God's relationship to the world, then Part Two explores the implications of that relationship. If the divine attribute of omnipotence, as classically understood, is replaced by omnipresence, as process theologians argue, then what are the ethical imperatives of that belief? It certainly isn't withdrawal from the world's concerns, nor is it withdrawal from even the more difficult issues of our day—evolution, abortion, stem cell research, global warming, and the 2008 collapse of the global financial market.

Beginning with his first book on the environmental crisis in 1972 (*Is It Too Late?*), John Cobb has exemplified his belief that theology is not restricted merely to matters of church doctrine but is vitally concerned with public life. What else would you expect from a process theologian, who sees God present in every moment of experience? When the natural sciences are "the water in which we swim," then theology must be in dialogue with science. When economics becomes the god of both politicians and populace, then theology must offer a language for both analysis and critique. When God is omnipresent, then we cannot escape the conclusion that whatever we do to or for "the least of these," we do it to God as well (Mt. 25:40).

In Part Three, attention turns more specifically to matters of faith. How does a process-relational theologian view incarnation? redemption? resurrection? What possible response can one give to the perennial problem of sin, suffering, and evil? It is here, especially, that process theology has much to contribute. The classically stated problem of evil is this: If God is all-good and all-powerful, why is there evil? If God could intervene, but doesn't "for our own good," then what do we do with truly horrendous evil? How can one *not* implicate God in human suffering if God is the giver of free will? As Dr. Cobb acknowledges, the problem of evil may be "the theological issue that confronts believers with the greatest personal urgency." (See chapter 7, p. 137.)

Most process theologians think that a process-relational theology provides the only satisfying response to these questions by leaving divine goodness intact and reframing divine power. As Dr. Cobb explains, the process God is not omnipotent. We, too, have the power of self-determination, of choice, as do those around us. All of these choices may land us in very precarious circumstances, as is the case with global warming, but in all of these choices God is also present, offering us the best possibility for that moment, calling us forward to a vision of well-being.

The remaining questions in Part Three contain some of Dr. Cobb's most personal statements about doctrine–its limits and possibilities–and faith. He shares his views on interreligious dialogue, for, again, an omnipresent God who is creatively and dynamically at work in the world is obviously not present in Christians only. A process-relational theology takes seriously the religious experiences and beliefs of others.

It has been many years since that seminar on the shores of Rainy Lake in northern Minnesota. Since then, it has been my honor and privilege to become a colleague and friend of John Cobb. Writer and philosopher, teacher and theologian, and servant of the church, he is a man of great intellect and the embodiment of graciousness. He is, quite simply, the preeminent process theologian in the world.

Through the lens of process thought, he has written on Christian doctrine and biblical interpretation, the environmental crisis, religious pluralism and interfaith dialogue, economics, evolution, and American public policy. Every month on the Process & Faith Web site, he answers questions–questions collected here for you–as diverse as the nature of God, the problem of evil, and intelligent design.

He is the beloved teacher of students all around the globe and the reason that many pastors are able to go back to the pulpit, Sunday after Sunday, and from the wreckage of the week preach a message of good news and the transforming power of God. We are, all of us, in his debt.

Jeanyne B. Slettom
Claremont, California
July 2009

PART ONE

Metaphysics

1

The Basics

Can you describe a Christian process theology in just a few pages?

Process theology does not have a single correct description. I am going to contrast it with some common patterns of Christian thinking and then make some positive statements on which almost all process theologians would agree.

Some Christians understand God primarily as lawgiver and judge. God is the one who has defined what is right and wrong, especially with respect to sexual morality. If one violates these rules, one may expect punishment either in this life or beyond.

Some Christians understand God as the one who controls everything, the Almighty or Omnipotent One. Accordingly, whatever happens must have a reason. That is, God must have a purpose for causing or permitting the event. For example, if a child is run over by a car, then God either wanted the child in heaven, needed to teach the parents a lesson, or saw that in the long run the death of the child was for the good of all.

Some Christians understand God as a powerful person with whom they may bargain. If they will perform the deeds they understand God wants, then God will take care of them or benefit them appropriately. Prayer can be a kind of negotiation with God.

Some Christians associate God very closely with Christianity. Only Christians know God and please God. Other people are the enemies of God unless they repent and become Christians. Sometimes this is more narrowly conceived as limiting God's approval to those Christians who understand God correctly, as one group defines correctness.

Some Christians associate God very closely with the well-being of their own people or nation. They may speak of loyalty to "God and country." They expect God to support the aims of their nation against others.

Some Christians think of God as truly masculine, even male. God's maleness supports the domination of women by men and the exclusion of women from priestly roles. Since men are more godlike than women, stereotypically masculine characteristics are honored more than stereotypically feminine ones. God is thought to act but not to be acted upon.

Some Christians think that the great majority of events can be fully understood without reference to God. They believe that, every now and again, God intervenes in the course of events. Their prayers are designed to persuade God to intervene to accomplish something they believe to be important.

Some Christians believe that God has a fixed plan for their lives. If they fail to follow it, God calls them back to it again and again. Once they agree to follow it, things will go well.

Some Christians believe that God has created human beings to rule the world. They believe that other creatures exist only for use by humans. The natural world is there to be exploited. This includes all the other animals. Their suffering is of no importance.

Process theology rejects all of these views. In doing so, it is not alone. Christian ecofeminists in particular share in these rejections and think in ways very congenial to process theology. Students of the Bible also often reject these views and come to conclusions similar to process theology without any direct influence. Hence, to explain the views of process theology is not to oppose all other theological approaches.

Speaking positively now, process theologians believe that the God revealed in Jesus' person and teaching is best understood in terms of love rather than of controlling power. This does not mean that God is powerless but that God's power is not coercive. We often say that God is persuasive, and that is correct. It may be still better to say that God's power is expressed in empowering creatures and giving them freedom as well as in calling them to express that freedom in love.

Process theologians believe that we cannot assume that what happens in the world is what God wants to have happen in the world. Each event is largely what it must be because of all the past events that inform it. God's role is to introduce the ability to be more than merely a deterministic outcome of the past. God thus liberates and provides direction. Even in this area, which displays some real freedom in the creature, God does not determine how that freedom is exercised. Otherwise it would not be freedom. In theological language, God's grace sets us free and guides us. It does not restrict us or compel us.

God's grace also saves us. This has multiple meanings. It saves us from sheer necessity and meaninglessness by endlessly offering us new possibilities for life and for becoming more alive. It makes possible solutions and breakthroughs in situations that seem hopeless. It enables us to hope for a positive future even when projections of present trends appear to lead to destruction.

God's grace is also radical empathy with us and acceptance of us, whatever we do with the opportunities God grants us. God takes us up into God's own life, and we live there forever. This is forgiveness and transformation. That means that everything we experience, God also experiences. God suffers with us as we suffer and rejoices with us as we rejoice. God understands as no other companion can. Soul and body cannot be separated. We are fully embodied souls and ensouled bodies. God loves our bodies as God loves our souls.

This means that God is in us and we are in God. God is a part of our very being, and we are parts of God's very being. It is quite literally true that in God we live and move and have our being. This is true not only of human beings but of all of God's creatures. What we do to the least of these, we do also to God.

The relationship between God and creatures is highly interactive. What God offers us in each moment depends on the situation in that moment. What God offers in the next moment depends on our response in the preceding one. God's "plan," if we can use that word at all, is continuously adjusted to the changing situation in the world.

This deep relationality is not only between creatures and God. It is also among creatures. In Paul's language, we are members one of another (1 Cor. 12:12–13). We do not exist as self-enclosed individuals but as social beings. We are what and who we are through our relationships with others.

Many of these others are, of course, human beings. We have no existence outside of human community. We are called to heal and strengthen human community and to oppose those forces that systematically weaken and undercut it. This has vast implications for economics and for social organization.

Our relations are also with the whole creaturely world. The well-being of the world contributes to our well-being, and its sickness and decay impoverish us as well. We seek the flourishing of other creatures for both their sake and ours. This has vast implications for the importance of our treatment of the natural world and our understanding of what policies are needed for a sustainable future.

Our opportunity and fulfillment is to love and serve God by loving and serving God's creatures. That does not mean that we must obey rules laid down by God. It means instead that we are to respond moment by moment to God's loving call to us. This is what it means to be faithful as Jesus was faithful. Because of Jesus, we can believe and trust and be assured of God's forgiveness and acceptance. We can hope for the salvation of the world and can work with God to that end.

Metaphysics seems remote and obscure. Do Christians really need to be concerned about it?

Obviously many believers of great faith have gotten along very well without thinking about metaphysics. I have emphasized "about" because I do not believe that anyone is totally free of metaphysical assumptions. Very early in life, each of us assimilates some ideas about what is real. Then our studies and additional socialization modify our thoughts. What we assimilate and are socialized into believing makes a lot of difference. Still, many people get along quite well without thinking about this dimension of their beliefs.

These deep-seated and rarely considered beliefs are of many sorts. If you have lived your whole life in the United States as a Euro-American, you are likely to have assimilated beliefs about the nature and history of the United States that are different from those you would take for granted if you had been brought up as a Native American or in China. These differences are not, at least primarily, metaphysical.

We also grow up with deeply embedded assumptions about what kinds of events are likely or even possible. Here, metaphysics does play a role. For example, some people easily accept the occurrence of mental telepathic communication. Others are quite convinced that it is not possible. The difference comes not from empirical evidence but from metaphysics. That is, some people see the world as one in which entities, or at least psyches, can act on one another from a distance. At the other extreme are those who fully accept the view of the world as a machine.

Neither of these views necessitates either affirming or denying God, but God's role is thought of differently in the two cases. Those who see creaturely psyches as interacting may think everything psychic or spiritual can be explained by this, or they may imagine that God, as cosmic psyche, interacts with all the creaturely psyches. Those who view the world as a great machine may consider the machine fully self-explanatory, or they may think that a machine requires an intelligent and powerful maker who is outside of it.

A person's views about the nature of reality depend on many things. To a large extent they depend on the beliefs and attitudes of those by whom one has been surrounded and on what one has heard and read. To some extent one's views of reality depend on individual critical reflection. This reflection will involve metaphysics, whether or not the one who reflects employs such a label.

Since the way we view reality is our metaphysics and since few of us think about it, the metaphysics that governs our thinking is largely determined socially and historically. Accordingly, some cultures support Christian faith in God, while others make such faith more difficult. The dominant culture of the twentieth century was an extreme case of one that discouraged such faith.

One major and influential expression of the dominant culture is the university. Its metaphysics is predominantly the mechanistic one noted earlier. By the twentieth century, the university, in the main, excluded the option of supposing that one should posit a creator of the machine. All events in the machine are to be understood in terms of the inner workings of the machine. God has no place to intervene. The university will not even accept the option that theists present when they accept the machine analogy but then argue that leaps in evolutionary development are better understood if we posit some purposeful force acting on the machine from without. Most Christian leaders in the declining old-line churches rush to the defense of the integrity of science.

Actually, the situation is still less favorable to faith than this suggests. The self-containedness of nature excludes not only God from having any role, but also animal, and even human, purpose. Scientists recognize, of course, that apparently purposeful human activity plays a large role in what happens today. They are pressed by their metaphysics to believe that ultimately all this is really explained mechanistically. In due course, they suppose, science will be able to explain human activity, including human thought, exclusively in terms of matter in motion, that is, of the machine as conceived in the seventeenth century. Meanwhile, as far as possible, they leave human activity out of the subject matter of the natural sciences.

I am not suggesting that anyone lives entirely by this metaphysics. I assume that living by this mechanistic metaphysics is impossible. This limitation reduces its power and opens up some space for faith to survive. Nevertheless, such faith in God has great difficulty articulating itself in a way that is convincing even to the faithful. Communities composed of believers of this sort are not likely to be able to act with great conviction.

A major response of philosophically informed theologians is the complete rejection of metaphysics. They do not mean that people fail to have beliefs about their world and how to live in it. They do mean that everyone should recognize that the "world" in question has no existence in itself. The supposition that the world, or God, exists independently of our beliefs about it is "metaphysical." As such, this supposition should be abandoned or outgrown. Instead, we should recognize that we live in a world of symbols whose meanings are exhausted by their relationship to other symbols. In the Abrahamic traditions, "God" is a centrally important symbol. Its meaning can be found in each Abrahamic tradition in its relations with other symbols. To be a Christian is to be socialized into this symbol system and to live in terms of it.

This response frees Christians from the dominance of the mechanistic worldview. That "world" is also seen as a system of symbols that do not refer to anything outside the symbol system. Christians should live in their symbol system and not in one adopted by some other community, such as that of scientists. Since none of our language refers to anything outside of language, there need be no conflict among such systems. In this form of thought, the question of truth either disappears or functions as one symbol among others, receiving its only meaning within particular symbol systems.

The study of symbol systems certainly proves illuminating, as does this understanding of Christian communities. Here I am making only one point. In the theistic traditions, including Christianity, prayer and worship, trust and devotion, have been directed to what, in these terms, is a metaphysical reality. That is, believers have understood that God is real quite independently of how they think of God. All that has been meant by "faith" has depended on this belief that the word "God" refers beyond language to another kind of reality. This is why raising the metaphysical question explicitly seems better than denying a priori that it is meaningful. It seems to me quite obvious that there are different ways of conceiving reality alongside the denial that there is anything beyond our language to which our language can refer. It also seems to me very clear that at least from the point of view of faith, our views on metaphysics are important. We should break the cultural taboo on such discussions.

Once we break that taboo, process philosophy has a good chance to make its case. When the seventeenth-century metaphysics that underlies most of what goes on in the university is brought fully to light as a metaphysic, it does not fare well. Gradually, the spell it has cast over the modern world can be broken. The inevitability of holding to some metaphysic may also become apparent. It may also be acknowledged that theistic metaphysics should be considered on a par with nontheistic ones.

These changes may sound rather simple. In fact they would be radical and revolutionary. I believe Christian faith has a stake in such a revolution.

How does process theology relate to the "new atheism"?

The intellectual-cultural context in which we operate favors atheism. Obviously, however, this does not lead most people to become atheists. In this culture, in its popular forms, "atheism" is still a negative word. It was associated with "communism," for example. Many people call themselves "agnostic" to avoid the label and also to acknowledge that certainty about what does not exist is unattainable.

Nevertheless, God has disappeared from the university. History books provide the evidence that people used to believe in God.

Courses in religious studies also can discuss the varied beliefs of people, some of which affirm God. But God cannot be included in the explanation of any event, historical or natural, and not even religious experience. The implication is that everything can be understood without reference to God. This assumes that any God who might exist plays no role in events.

More recently, God has been excluded from public education as well. This is partly because teachers are educated in the university where they learn to exclude God from any role in what happens. Another factor is society's increasing religious diversity, which makes the introduction of religious ideas or practices threaten to favor one community over others. The solution is to exclude all religious talk or practice from the schools. Of course, teachers may teach about them, but they should not teach their beliefs as truths. This includes belief that there is God.

Theology is taught at the college or university level only in Catholic and conservative Protestant institutions. Much of what I say would need to be considerably qualified in its application to these schools. Liberal Protestant schools and private ones do not allow theology unless they have attached seminaries. Even in seminaries, very little role is assigned to God. Historians and biblical scholars will discuss the role of belief in God more than their historical peers in other areas, and they may emphasize its importance to a greater extent. But their understanding of historical scholarship differs little from that of secular historians. It is rare, indeed, that professors in these fields will suggest that God actually affects the course of events. The discussion of this possibility is left to professors of theology.

Even theologians experience some embarrassment about this topic. They offer a variety of responses. A traditional one consists in the idea that we can distinguish the primary and secondary causes of events. Science and historical study deal with secondary causes. These leave no gaps. However, this seamless account as a whole is compatible with the view that God is the primary cause of all that happens. University professors find no need to mention this unless one is asking specifically religious questions.

Sometimes the primary causality can be associated with Being as such. Thomas Aquinas wrote of *esse ipsum;* Heidegger of *sein selbst.* In other words, the being of all that is derives from God, although God is not a factor influencing the forms that being takes. This is explained exhaustively by natural and historical causes.

Another solution has been to bifurcate knowledge. Immanuel Kant is the most influential source of this way of thinking. German universities reflect this way of thinking in the sharp distinction between the *Naturwissenschaften* and the *Geisteswissenschaften*. For Kant, God cannot possibly play a role in the former, but in reflections about ethics and in theology itself, the postulate of God makes sense. With few exceptions, however, those who have adopted the bifurcation have found ways to discuss ethics without recourse to God. Theology, however, can still be claimed as a sphere within which God, and even God's actions, can be affirmed without impinging on the territory of the sciences.

From Kant one may go all the way to a pure idealism, that is, the idea that only mind exists. For him the existence of a physical world depends on the ordering of sense-data by the mind. The role he assigned to an independent nature is very limited and, given his general position, difficult to defend. Accordingly, many of his followers attributed reality only to the mind. Christian Science stands in this tradition and draws its implications practically although most philosophical idealists do not.

In the twentieth century, many theologians have rejected metaphysics entirely. For some of them, such as Karl Barth, this has meant affirming the biblical worldview in which God is central without connecting it in any way to philosophical grounding. For most in the latter part of the twentieth century and the present, this has meant instead that all we have to think about is the world of language and symbols. "God" is important here, but we cannot discover a way to go from the word to some reality that exists independently of it. The utterance of the word can have some causal effect, but this does not attribute any role to the reality it has traditionally named.

Another option has been to locate God in the future. For example, God can be identified with the ultimate destiny of all things, a destiny that is implicitly anticipated by human beings. In this way, God exercises causal efficacy in the present but not in such a way as to compete with the kinds of causes studied by scientists and historians.

In contrast with all of this, popular belief and conservative theology affirm God as causally effective in the world. Since all events are thought to be caused by other events and to be obedient to natural laws, the image of such divine action is necessarily supernatural. God supernaturally created the world and supernaturally acts in the world. It is this supernaturalism against which the university organizes itself. To allow it would be to disrupt the whole program of science and history.

The argument about a God who really does something and makes a difference, therefore, is generally initiated by theists pointing to something that cannot be explained in a natural way. This has been particularly important in relation to evolutionary theory. The coming into being of life out of inanimate matter, or complex forms of life out of simple ones, and of subjective experience out of mere objects seems to require miraculous interventions. These claims stir biologists to show that such developments can be explained in naturalistic terms. Even if they admit they do not have complete explanations now, they point to the many gaps, previously viewed as inexplicable naturalistically, that have in time been filled by scientists. They also argue that positing an act of God is not science and cannot be integrated into a scientific explanation. Since such a theory is "theology" rather than science, and since theology cannot be taught outside of theological schools, any reference to God is in principle barred from an explanatory role anywhere else.

In this intellectual-cultural context, atheistic biologists have considerable advantage over their theistic critics. They have on their side the whole university culture and the whole community of scientists. Individual scientists may personally believe in God, but their science excludes God from any role. Those who try to introduce God as a causal agent are not providing one hypothesis among others to be considered but are rejecting science as such as it is currently understood, taught, and practiced. If one thinks that belief in God, or at least in any God who makes a difference in the world, depends on finding some supernatural events, the likely result is atheism.

Let us turn now to the distinctive approach of process thought. Process thought continues the effort to understand reality, including God, as given for us rather than as simply part of our language. However, it rejects both materialism and supernaturalism. It criticizes both the science that is bound up with materialism and its theological critics who propose a supernaturalist alternative.

Scientists and supernaturalists accept the same view of the natural world, namely, that of Descartes. By the eighteenth century, science had wedded itself to the mechanistic view of what it studied. Its conservative Christian critics do not dispute this mechanistic metaphysics, and they are, accordingly, forced to present their alternatives in a supernatural fashion. If the world is a machine, it is composed of matter in motion. Matter has no interiority. Accordingly, matter can be acted on only externally. Since its only behavior is motion, God would have to be thought of as moving matter in a way that conflicts with the forces and laws already operative. Newton thought this occurred, but for at least two hundred years now, science has excluded it. Such an act of God is, in any case, very difficult to imagine. Process theology has no place for it.

The process alternative can be stated very simply. The entities that make up the world have interiority. That is, they are something in and for themselves and do not exist only objectively for others. This is hardest for many to accept when we talk of elementary entities such as quanta, but with respect to biology, it is enough to speak of living things. We do in fact believe that not only other human beings but also our pets and other animals are subjects as well as objects.

The process critique of evolutionary theory, accordingly, does not begin by seeking a gap in explanation that we fill with God, but gaps that we fill by the actions of animals. Notice that I say "actions" rather than behavior. Behavior can, on an a priori basis, be assumed to be the result of matter in motion, but the word "action" points to behavior that is harder to subsume into the matter-in-motion paradigm. When we think of an action, we think of something intentional rather than of something that is simply the outward manifestation of the chance or necessary motions of matter. Behavior can be viewed as simply objective. Action involves the subject. That the actions of animals have an effect on the course of evolution is an assertion for which there is a great deal of evidence, even though it is ignored in standard theories of evolution.

The point of all of this is that the sciences exclude the subjective side of reality almost as completely as they exclude God. These two exclusions are closely related. Although people sometimes think of creation and the imposition of law, as well as miracles, as acts of God on the objective world, the great majority of religious thinking deals with how God works in subjective experience. Even Jesus' healings, which one might suppose occur in the objective world, are attributed by him to subjective states, especially to faith. Whereas any effort to image God's acts objectively tends to evoke our own incredulity, imaging God's call and grace and judgment in our subjective experience has considerable verisimilitude. That God influences the subjective experience of other animals as well as human beings is a reasonable judgment.

Access to the world of objectivity with which science deals is through the sense organs. Sensory empiricism is, accordingly, closely related to science. This kind of empiricism actually provides us no idea of causality, or natural law, or even temporality. Immanuel Kant understood this and proposed that causality, natural law, and temporality are given by the structure of the human mind. Whitehead showed that causality, natural law, and temporality are given, or derivative from what is given, in our subjective experience. So are novelty and freedom, as well as the sense of better and worse. He shows that we have nonsensory perception that is more basic than that which is mediated by sense organs. In the analysis of this subjective world, excluded by science, God plays an important role.

Process thinkers believe that what happens subjectively affects what happens objectively and that excluding the subject from the study of living things leads science to incomplete explanations. This is especially true where human beings are involved, but it is true also of other animals. When animals learn new ways of procuring food or enter into symbiotic relations, the selection of mutated genes is affected. Evolutionists rarely deny this, but they do not include it in standard accounts of evolution.

Unless and until the extensive role of animal subjectivity in evolution is acknowledged and included in the account of evolution, evolutionary theory will be thoroughly atheistic and also morally nihilistic. Giving the subjective lives of animals their due place will not automatically lead to theism, but the fullest and deepest account of what transpires in subjectivity, moment by moment, involves the creaturely relationship to God. This relationship grounds both order and novelty, both law and freedom. Through it God influences, but does not determine, what happens in the world.

What is the process view of angels and demons?

On the whole, we process theologians developed our theologies at a time when individual angels and individual demons were little considered in theological circles. Accordingly, we have thought and written almost nothing about them.

On the other hand, the idea of demonic powers, of "principalities and powers," was profoundly important. Shaped by a period in which Italy followed the fascist Mussolini, and the most highly educated country in the world, Germany, followed Hitler, when advanced technology was used to commit genocide, and when the world as a whole was drawn into the mutual slaughter of war, it was not possible to ignore the historical power of evil. The liberal notion of historical progress, with education and technology as the solutions to all our problems, looked absurdly wrong. To explain historical evil simply in terms of individuals falling short of God's call was completely unconvincing in light of what was happening. Clearly, powers of another kind were at work! Some of us followed Paul Tillich in calling them demonic.

That does not mean that we viewed human beings as helpless victims of these powers. Process theologians emphasize that every person in every moment has some freedom and responsibility. Nevertheless, at the same time we emphasize that for the most part we are constituted in each moment by our past. Whitehead called this past one's "actual world." That actual world contains much that is good, but it also contains much that is evil.

An example may help to clarify what I mean. The actual world of most Christians, especially in Europe, contained negative views of Jews. The gospel of John places the assertion on the lips of Jesus that the Jews are children of the devil. In general the gospels blame them for the crucifixion of Jesus. Both of these facts reflect a situation in which followers of Jesus were persecuted by mainstream Jews. During the period when both Jews and Christians were persecuted by Rome, their quarrel had relatively minor consequences, but when the empire became Christian, these consequences became historically of great importance. They included long-term persecution accompanied by periodic pogroms. The worse the treatment of Jews by Christians, the more important it became for Christians to justify themselves by inventing stories about the evil of Jews. Because Jews were assigned the role of money lenders, they acted in ways that further exacerbated Christian feelings.

Those growing up in this cultural climate inherited hostility to Jews quite apart from any personal experience of them. For many, the word "Jew" seemed derogatory in itself. The presence of Jews in society was felt as a threat. If they were economically successful, this was attributed to sinister methods.

In other words, anti-Judaism became a powerful force in Western society largely independent of individuals and their personal judgments. Of course, a few Christians could criticize and transcend this aspect of their "actual worlds" to some extent. None could be altogether unaffected by this anti-Judaism. For hundreds of years anti-Judaism has constituted a demonic element in Christendom. Further, as nationalism succeeded Christianity as the primary unifying commitment of Western societies, this demonic force persisted. In the aftermath of World War II, the churches came to recognize their responsibility for Nazi genocide, leading to real efforts to exorcise this demonic power from our cultures. Some progress has been made, but Jews rightly sense that the demon has not been fully destroyed. They remain fearful of the potential for this "demon" to be awakened and attack them yet again.

This is an example of pervasive attitudes and feelings structured into language and culture. In other instances the demonic takes institutional form. In my opinion, many of our political and economic institutions embody demonic power. When this institutionalization is combined with a supporting culture and language, as is often the case, the demons are even harder to exorcise.

For process theologians, the identification and exorcism of demonic forces of this kind is more important than reflection about demons in the sense of malevolent personal spirits. Nevertheless, I do not want to reject or belittle the question. Can process thought allow for the actual existence of angels and demons?

My answer here is that, yes, it can. I will begin with demons. In principle, it is not impossible that there are spirits without the sort of bodies that we possess who nevertheless act destructively on us and in us. The metaphysics of Whitehead, as such, did not exclude this. Since the New Testament takes demon possession for granted, theologians do need to engage this idea.

In the modern period, the most common response to the New Testament account has been to assert that it is a primitive explanation of various psychoses. One psychosis that can easily lend itself to this explanation is that of dual personalities. The most famous fictional account is of Dr. Jekyll and Mr. Hyde. To say that when Dr. Jekyll becomes Mr. Hyde he has been possessed by an evil spirit is not far from the truth. Nevertheless, a contemporary psychological account, or the explanation in terms of drugs, is more convincing and more helpful for therapy.

Traditional Catholic circles encourage psychological study while believing that, in certain cases, demon possession is the accurate diagnosis and exorcism is the correct response. Certainly, in many instances in Africa today this diagnosis is made, and exorcism seems effective. I am perhaps too much of a child of modernity to be fully convinced. But I do not exclude the possibility.

If instances of literal demon possession occur, what are the demons? One possibility would be that they are the spirits of persons who have died but whose anger or jealousy is so great that they are not willing or able to leave Earth. They establish a relation to the brain of some living person without disconnecting from their previous past. They may alternate in dominance over the body with its own soul or they may fully subordinate that soul. I confess that I find such speculations implausible, but I also understand that there are well-documented instances in which something of this sort seems to fit the reported facts.

Turning to angels, I think it might be helpful to start with Whitehead's idea of different grades of actual entities. His account is very technical, but I believe that I can give a roughly comparable set of distinctions in more easily understood fashion.

The lowest grade of occasions—momentary unconscious experiences—consists of occasions in empty space. They are just as actual as any other occasions, but they lack the patterns of relationships that provide stability. They do not form societies that endure through time, even short periods of time. They constitute the energy that physicists have found exists even in a vacuum.

The second grade of occasions comprises those that do form societies. The existence of these societies means that the space is no longer empty. These societies make up the inanimate objects that constitute so much of our universe. These include subatomic entities as well as the gases, liquids, and solids of which we are more likely to think. Photons belong to this grade.

The third grade of occasions consists in those that comprise societies in which life plays a significant role. No completely clear line demarcates between animate and inanimate occasions, but the differences in individual occasions can be magnified or diminished in the societies to which they belong. For the most part the distinction between the animate and the inanimate is clear and important.

The final grade of occasions makes up the subjective experience of creatures like ourselves. Here the mental element, which is present in all occasions, is canalized in such a way that what is novel in one occasion is transmitted to the next and enlarged there. Learning takes place. In some cases, consciousness arises. Our own partly conscious experience provides us the only immediate access to considering what an actual occasion is like.

God does not appear in this list, because Whitehead said God is the one entity that is not an actual occasion. God is everlasting, whereas an occasion is momentary. Adding God, we could say that Whitehead differentiated five grades of actual entities.

In Whitehead's account, nothing is said about a grade, such as angels, coming between human beings and God. He did very tangentially suggest the possibility that the human psyche could exist separately from the human body. That would not, for him, necessarily constitute a different grade of occasion, but we could easily consider it so. I mention this not to say that Whitehead affirmed anything of this sort but to remind us of the openness of his cosmology. His attention was focused on those things about which we have strong evidence. His philosophy did not preclude the existence of other things as well. Should there be good reason to affirm the reality of angels, a process theologian should do so.

On the other hand, process thought does not point toward the reality of angels. Angels came into the religious imagination of people largely because they felt that God was too remote to relate to them directly. Messengers were needed. For process thought, God is immediately involved in every occasion. No space remains for an intermediary.

A second basis for affirming angels comes from visions. The idea of angels as beings of light is certainly associated with these visions. That experiences of light have played a large role in the history of religions is indubitable. Again, the question is how these are to be interpreted. At one extreme are reductive explanations in terms of the stimulus of a particular region of the brain. For a Whiteheadian, the question is what stimulates that region, leading to the projection of a vision? There is no reason to deny that the stimulus is divine. Again, do we need a creature as the stimulus, or can that be God?

A third reason for belief in angels is a sense of too large a gap between earthly creatures and God in the great chain of beings. Angels could fill a vacant slot. Process thought senses no need to fill such a gap. Process theologians take evolutionary thought seriously, even if we criticize the dominant neo-Darwinian theory. When people assumed the separate creation of humans, they made it easy to suppose a separate creation of angels. When we understand the higher grades of occasions to have arisen out of the lower ones, the idea of a separate creation of angels seems implausible.

Again, I emphasize that process thought is not dogmatic about what does not exist. The point is simply that its reading of the cosmos and of religious experience does not lead in the direction of angels. As of now, we think that human beings must take full responsibility for their lives and are called and empowered by God to do so. Expecting help from angels can distract from our responsibilities. We process theologians believe that relying directly on God's grace is the more fully Christian practice.

Angels are supposed to be messengers of God. I believe that in a broad sense we are all called to be angels. But for most people, the question about angels is understood in a narrower sense. Are there spirits without bodies like ours who do God's bidding and seek our good? Perhaps. If so, how did they come into being?

Once again, if I speculate about such possibilities, I incline to think of them as human beings who have died. Unlike demons, angels do not take possession of people. They act, in good process fashion, persuasively. I would not draw a sharp line among the sense of the continuing presence and aid of loved ones who have recently died, the idea that saints may intercede for us, and the ministration of angels. Before trying to formulate a theory of angels, however, we need to consider critically the evidence for their reality. The fact that in comparison with dominant habits of modern thought, Whitehead opened a door to types of reality that had long been excluded, does not mean that every idea popular in religious circles is true or beneficial. The diagnosis of a problem such as demon possession can lead to treatments that cause great suffering with no beneficial consequences.

My own judgment is that Christian theology is better off without literal inclusion of angels. Talk of angels usually reflects a view of God as external and distant. Why does God send a messenger? Does that not imply that God is somewhere else, not present here and now? For many Christians, and certainly for process thinkers, God is very near indeed. God is continuously alive within us. Why should we talk about messengers when God speaks constantly to us? Similarly, the idea that God assigns us guardian angels implies that God is not able to attend to us directly and personally. Process theology understands God as directly and personally within us.

Another danger looms in taking angels and demons seriously. We are all familiar with the line, "The devil made me do it." I have emphasized at the outset that much of the reason for the evil we do can be found in demonic power. We need to take responsibility for allowing such power to dominate us. God calls us to transcend and oppose it. Thinking of demons as having the potential to control us works against this acceptance of personal responsibility.

Sometimes people even picture themselves as the battleground between an angel and a demon. They are almost passive in this picture, waiting to see which spirit wins. It is better to think of the past out of which we are largely constituted as containing much good and much evil, and of God as calling us to fulfill the best of its potentialities, thus changing what we pass on to our future selves and to others as their actual world. We don't need personalized demons and angels to describe our condition.

In First Samuel, we find that Saul outlawed mediumship. This was not a matter of disbelief in the powers of mediums. When he wanted to consult the then-deceased Samuel, he found a medium to establish communication. The objection to mediumship was that we should relate directly to God, and that suffices. I think this is good advice to us—not as a law that has no exceptions but as a general recommendation. Spiritually, I see very little that we can gain by thinking about angels and demons, whereas I do see a good deal of potential danger. I think it possible that entities really exist to which these terms appropriately apply. I am open to the evidence. Without convincing evidence, so far as I am concerned, nothing of Christian importance is lost.

I wonder whether the vastly increased interest in angels in the past few decades reflects a loss of personal experience of God. If that is so, and if talk of angels helps to restore even an indirect personal relationship, I should not be so critical. Would it not be better, however, to think and write of the working of the Holy Spirit or of the living Christ and to encourage the sense of that presence in our lives? Certainly that emphasis would bring us more closely in line with Paul's thought.

Where does process theology stand on the issue of free will?

Process theology affirms self-determination but not "free will." That may seem like a quibble, but it is an important quibble. The idea of the "will" is part of a way of thinking that process theology rejects. It is sometimes called "faculty psychology," which views the mind as a collection of separate modules assigned to different tasks. Faculty psychology depicts the human psyche as divided into quasi-substantial parts—for example, passion, reason, and will.

Freud's analysis of the psyche in terms of id, ego, and superego is another example.

The objection to faculty psychology is not that these terms have no meaningful referents. The problem is that they reify aspects of the total psychic life and compartmentalize these reified elements. The will is one of these reified elements. After its existence is questionably established, then the question arises whether it is bound by the passions, or by reason, or is free. The further question arises as to whether freedom is synonymous with "uncaused" or "arbitrary." If so, freedom hardly provides a basis for moral responsibility.

Obviously, other philosophies and theologies can provide answers to my questions that work fairly well, but this whole approach is alien to process thought. Faculty psychology has never been successful in explaining human freedom. Process theologians, in contrast, understand the psyche to be a succession of moments, or occasions of experience. Each occasion derives from God an aim that guides its integration of its past. The aim is also adjusted during this process. The exact outcome is not determined until it happens.

In Whitehead's view, everything about the outcome is then determined, but there are multiple determinants. Much of the outcome is determined by the past occasions that are synthesized. This is the causality studied by scientists. Some of it is determined by the contribution of God. Even the combined influence of the past and of God does not determine exactly what the outcome will be. This is the "decision" of that occasion itself. Hence self-determination plays a role. Whitehead said that every occasion is in part *causa sui,* cause of itself. This is also the choosing discussed in the preceding section.

Self-determination provides a meaningful way to understand "freedom." The problem with "freedom" is that it can be understood negatively. That is, "freedom" is often understood only to mean "not determined." If that is the case, an outcome would seem to be a matter of sheer chance. What is self-determined is that which is not determined by the past or by God but by the occasion itself. If freedom means simply not determined at all, then neither the occasion nor the person of whom it is a part is responsible for the outcome. If the outcome is determined by the occasion itself, then there is responsibility.

This idea of self-determination has been very difficult to articulate outside the process conceptuality. It is the idea of the process being made up of successive occasions that makes self-determination meaningful. Consider the problem.

Ordinary conceptions of causality require that the cause precede the effect. When the flow of events is understood as a continuum, however close the cause is to the effect, there is no "present" in which a decision about itself can be made. For this reason, the great majority of discussions of freedom have equated it with indeterminism. The discovery of indeterminism at the quantum level has been regarded as supportive of the identification of freedom and indeterminism. Other philosophers point out that believing there is random, uncaused behavior is of no use in explaining the human awareness of freedom.

The view that the course of events takes place through successive actual occasions opens the door to another kind of reflection. A person could still argue that the occasion is fully determined by its past. Just how the event integrates that past would then be entirely the result of what the past is. This is a conceptually plausible view. For a long time it seemed that physicists were demonstrating its adequacy for the natural world. Evolutionary theory extended it to the understanding of human beings as well.

The advocates of this kind of determinism generally acknowledge that along with the factual past we require some kind of physical laws to explain what happens. The use of the term "laws" reminds us that for centuries people assumed that these laws presupposed a lawgiver, namely, God. Accordingly, the full explanation of what happened required appeal not only to the factual past but also to God. As time passed, scientists felt less and less need to attribute the "laws" they discovered to a lawgiver who was distinct from the laws. The regularities identified in the laws could be thought of as a matter of chance, but the door to a theistic explanation has never been closed. Recent discoveries have called attention to the "constants" that make life possible in this universe, but could so easily have been different. The theistic explanation has regained some traction.

However, an explanation of what happens in the occasion that is comprised only of the factual past and God still seems to provide no room for self-determination. This requires another step. God's role must be understood as providing alternative ways of synthesizing the past rather than determining exactly what the synthesis will be. Whitehead proposed that we think of a divine ordering of potentiality that provides laws but also alternatives. Every way of synthesizing the past that God makes possible will illustrate the laws of physics. But there are many ways, not just one, to synthesize the past. Of the several ways an occasion can actualize itself, all but one must be rejected. In other words, the occasion "decides" uniquely.

This goes some distance to account for the sense of responsibility for what we do and become, but it is still not sufficient. If the options among which the occasion chooses are morally equal, the decision has no moral value. For humans, the connection of freedom and morality is very close.

Whitehead proposed that the options derived from God are "graded" in terms of the value attained by actualizing them. In other words, some options are better than others. In his book on religion, Whitehead expressed the view that in all cultures one finds some sense of having partly realized and partly missed the way, the ideal possibility, the maximum value–what he there called "the rightness in things." He gave us an account of God's dealing with us that explained how it is possible for us to have that sense. We decide in response to God's call. That call may be to act in a way that seems to us too risky or too costly. We are likely to compromise between the full realization of the possibility to which we are called and something that feels more secure or more comfortable or more satisfying. Hence we also sense that we are responsible both for what we have achieved and for having, in biblical language, "missed the mark."

I believe that a sound philosophical grounding of our common experience of responsible freedom requires all of these steps. First, actual entities must act in their own constitution. Second, there must be limited but real options in the way in which the past functions in constituting these entities. Third, such options can only come from outside the occasion, and their source is properly called God. Fourth, these options must be graded, so that some are better than others.

Whitehead has provided us a conceptuality that includes all of these elements. He was guided in doing so by his conviction that in fact all of us believe that we do have some responsibility for how we act and who we become. We need a philosophy that does not deny these ineradicable beliefs. The task of philosophy is to explain rather than to explain away. Process theologians are deeply grateful to Whitehead for having provided us a way of understanding and confidently reaffirming our sense of responsible freedom.

Of course, many people are content to affirm their moral responsibility for what they do without engaging in philosophical reflection. Even those who subscribe to theories that deny any such responsibility cannot eradicate their sense of responsibility altogether. Nevertheless, we are disturbed that academic study generally instills deterministic ways of thinking and provides little support for our sense of self-determination and resultant responsibility. As more and more people are socialized to think in this way, the cultural climate changes. Young people are more likely to excuse themselves for their failures than to strive for moral excellence.

For Christians, however, it is important not to leave matters at this level. Three problems come with giving primacy to morality. First, people find it all too easy to assume responsibility for features of a situation for which they in fact have little or no responsibility. For psychic and social health, it is as important to analyze accurately the limits of responsibility as to affirm its reality.

Second, people face a grave danger, rarely completely avoided, of confusing the call of God with the social code of the local society. Such codes are generally helpful and even necessary. But they often include elements that are deeply hurtful. The call of God may be to break with elements of inherited moral teaching.

Third, our value and meaning as human beings is not finally derived from our morality. Jesus emphasized that repentant sinners enter God's realm ahead of those who are "righteous." Love counts for much more than moral virtue. Or perhaps to express matters better, true righteousness consists in responsiveness to the call of God. Although this call and response give rise to an understanding of what we usually understand as moral responsibility, they go beyond that. More fundamentally, and more ultimately, God calls for faith, hope, and love. These "theological virtues" both ground and relativize morality.

Also, we are most free when we allow God's call to work in us as grace giving us what we will receive. Our freedom is not greatest, therefore, when we struggle to decide rightly. The freedom we feel when we are consciously making decisions is not the highest form of freedom. We are most free when we are most open to what God gives us, when our self-determination is least distinct from God's causality within us.

How does process theology account for the uniqueness of the human person?

The question could mean either what distinguishes human persons from other animals or what distinguishes them from one another. I am assuming that the latter question is in view. The quick and easy answer to this question would be to say that each person is unique because no two people have the same genetic endowment (except identical twins) or the same environment, and no two people make the same choices. Indeed, that is the answer of process thought, and many people will readily nod their heads in agreement. But the problems involved in making this assertion are complex.

Most of the public debate is about the relative importance of heredity and environment. The importance of personal choices is rarely considered. This is largely because the academy encourages us to explain personal choices in terms of heredity and environment. To list them as a distinct explanation, while seeming reasonable to many, is rare among scientists and scholars. Insistence that choice is truly a factor, without questioning the importance of both heredity and environment as well, is a distinctive feature of process thought. Indeed, for process thinkers, if persons are to be explained entirely in terms of heredity and environment, they are in fact not persons at all, but automata. Accordingly, my answer will focus on how real choice is explained in this perspective.

The difficulty in affirming choice is rooted in the substance thinking that shapes our Indo-European languages. We are led to think that if there is choice, there is something that exists prior to the choice that does the choosing. You choose, or I choose. Then it seems that the reason you or I, our underlying "selves," choose as we do is because of who we are, and who we are is explained by heredity and environment. The power of our language in shaping our thought is such that any other way of understanding choice seems hard to understand.

Two and a half millennia ago, the Buddhists faced a similar problem in India. There a different Indo-European language had created a strong sense of the self, or atman. Reflection on that atman had led some Indian thinkers to the view that the self that acts in all things is not affected by its actions. Actually, it has no qualities at all. It turns out to be identical with Brahman or being, as such. In other words, the analysis of the substance underlying personal thought and action showed that this substance was the same as that underlying everything else, that it was immutable and eternal and undifferentiated. The religious result, before the Buddhists, tended to be a depreciation of the importance of all that is differentiated. All that happens, all that becomes, all that changes belongs to the world of appearance rather than the world of reality.

Buddhists made an opposite move. They decided that no such undifferentiated substance underlies all particulars. The particulars and their flux of change constitute the whole of reality. These particulars are events rather than substances. Some of these events are human experiences.

If that is the case, these events are not happening *to* something more fundamental. They *are* the reality. Human experiences are not experiences belonging to an underlying self. They constitute the self. These experiences are the way the world comes together in that location. Buddhists spoke of *pratitya samutpada,* often translated "dependent origination" (nothing exists independently of other things). The experience is the integration of the whole world.

I have described the form of Buddhist thought that Whitehead's philosophy most nearly approximated. He added a point that is very important for Christians. The integration can occur in more than just one way. The past does not decide which possible path will be taken. This is decided only in the occurrence itself.

So who or what decides? In Whitehead's language, the actual occasion of experience decides. That does not mean that the actual occasion first comes into being and then decides. The actual occasion can only come into being through the decision.

Similarly, an actual occasion does not first exist and then prehend other occasions. The actual occasion is the outcome of its prehensions. To bring this out, Whitehead spoke of the occasion as superject. However, to avoid the implication of complete causal determination by the past, he said it is a subject-superject.

This analysis applies to the quanta studied by physicists as well as to human experiences. It is interesting that quantum physicists sometimes speak of the "decisions" in that realm. Whitehead made clear that he used the word in its root meaning of "cutting off." Among the multiple possibilities, only one is realized. This is true for the quantum events and it is true for human beings. Which one is realized is decided neither by past occasions nor by God. It is decided in the coming to be of the occasion and only there. This is the grounds of the radical indeterminacy in the world. Whitehead thought that what is indeterminacy for the observer is self-determination for the occasions involved. At the human level this self-determination underlies the sense of responsibility for what we do.

The answer to the question of who or what decides is this: The occasion decides, but only in and through the decision does it complete itself. Concrescence is an activity that brings an entity into being. Concrescence is the activity of that entity in the process of creating itself. Indeed, it is that process of self-creation. This process includes a selection of one way to be among possible ways of being.

I am being repetitive, but since the notion of some completed thing doing the thinking or the acting is so deeply entrenched, it seems important to repeat the alternative description several times. The occasion does decide. That is the answer to the question. But if one simply says that, the habit of substance thinking will transform that answer into the picture of an occasion fully existing and then deciding. In that case it cannot decide what it will be–only what, with its being decided, it will do. The logic of this thought form will return us to a comprehensive deterministic vision.

If we are to have a metaphysical basis for affirming human freedom, we must assert that entities participate in deciding what they will be. That is self-determination. There can be self-determination only if deciding is part of the process of becoming what the entity uniquely becomes.

So far I have simply followed Whitehead. I think we may speculate somewhat further with respect to how this process transpires in highly evolved occasions such as human experiences. My judgment is that this varies somewhat among individuals and even among cultures. I wrote a book in which I speculated about the diversity of what I called "structures of human existence." I suspect that in different structures of existence, the decision occurs somewhat differently.

For most adults in the sphere of influence of the Abrahamic traditions, personal identity develops strongly through time. We think of ourselves as the same persons we were in infancy and will be if we are afflicted with Alzheimer's disease. Even with us, this is qualified somewhat. We can speak of conversion making us new persons. Disease, especially disease affecting the brain, can lead us to say of someone that she is not the same person she used to be. Cases of multiple personality confuse our talk of personal identity. Most of the time we ignore all of these qualifications and assume that one, and only one, person is associated with a human body and that this one person is identical from birth to death and perhaps from before death to after life. This assumption is connected to the substance thinking that sharply distinguishes the primary reality from the changing experience, behavior, and character.

Process thought rejects this view but must account for the strong sense of identity most of us feel through long stretches of time. I judge that this is based on the primacy, moment after moment, of the prehension of antecedent moments of personal experience. That is, my personal past flows into each successive moment of my life along with other entities, but I feel my personal past more intensely. Phenomenologically, in this structure of existence, the occasion does not experience itself as simply integrating numerous diverse prehensions. It experiences itself as integrating experiences of "other" entities with its personal past. The self or "I" is the continuation of that personal past. The occasion anticipates successor occasions that continue that personal line. The decision will be how other prehensions and anticipations are integrated with the prehension of the personal past and the anticipation of the personal future. We could almost say that the decision is made by this prehension and anticipation–but we should not say that. The decision is made in the process of the concrescence of the occasion in which this prehension and anticipation play the role of "self."

Buddhists engage in meditational practices designed to reduce the role in the present of the personal past and future. To whatever extent they are successful, the process of decision will be different. Self will not be so sharply differentiated from other. There will be a greater tendency for the whole of the past to play a less differentiated role in constituting the present.

Western mystics may function in a way quite different from most Christians and most Buddhists. They seek unity with God. In terms of Whitehead's categories, God's presence in the occasion, or the occasion's prehension of God, becomes the primary reality in the occasion. The distinction between God's decision and the creaturely one fades.

We could distinguish the experience of tribal people. We could also talk about the experience of the Jewish prophets. We can speculate, as I have done in my Christology, about the structure of Jesus' experience and that of Paul. These are possible uses of Whitehead's conceptuality to relate it to the multiplicity of forms of human experience. But it is important not to confuse such speculations with the metaphysical judgment that, in all cases, decision is the final stage of concrescence of all actual entities.

We might use different ways to answer the question as to who makes the decision. In the sphere of influence of the Abrahamic traditions, for most people the personal self primarily makes the decision. For advanced Buddhists, it is made by the totality of things. For theistic mystics, it is made by God. This only means that in the process of concrescence these data of prehension play primary roles.

Is it really possible to think this way? Buddhists found it very difficult. They criticized conceptual thought in general and strove to liberate themselves from it. In an appropriate meditative state, they thought, people could be released from the power of concepts and let reality be what it is.

David Bohm was convinced that substance thought inhibited the advance of science. He rightly noted that even when the expectations arising from substance thinking are dramatically refuted by the evidence, scientists tend to invent new substance concepts rather than abandon the language of substance. He devoted some time to developing a language based on gerunds rather than nouns. He believed, rightly I think, that if we were accustomed to hearing a gerund like "deciding" used as the subject of most sentences we would be less likely to look for a substance that decides.

Contemporary deconstructive postmodernism engages in elaborate linguistic exercises to break the power of deeply entrenched habits of thought. It shares with Buddhism and process thought the rejection of substances and especially of "the self" as a substance. It has influenced a significant segment of the academic community, but it remains quite esoteric for most people. It "deconstructs" much that needs deconstruction, but as with the Buddhists it does not develop an alternative conceptuality.

Whitehead differed on this latter point. He did offer a new vocabulary. For this he was often criticized. However, the difficulty in understanding him is not nearly as much the learning of a different vocabulary as entering into a different sense of what is real.

It may be that the linguistic changes that Whitehead made were not drastic enough. It is too easy to treat "prehensions" and "occasions" as if they were themselves substance-like. Whitehead was not free of this tendency himself. His interpreters, and I include myself, have generally made matters worse. Perhaps someday a Buddhist writer on Whitehead, one who is truly free from substantialist habits of mind, might carry Whitehead's revolutionary work further. I am sure that Whitehead would be pleased.

In answer to the question of what makes each human person unique, I have referred to the obvious importance of heredity and environment, but because these factors in explanation are not controversial, I have focused on a third factor, choice, in terms of *persons,* the most important of all. I have argued that choices cannot be finally explained by heredity and environment. But to do so I have had to deal with Whitehead's fundamental metaphysics, his radical rejection of substance in favor of events and processes. It is only by making this profound philosophical move that the commonsense belief that in part we choose who we will be can be rescued from the determinism that is built into most modern science.

2

God

The issue of immanence and transcendence is crucial for religious thought. One reason that it never gets settled is that it has so many meanings and turns up in so many different contexts. A view that emphasizes immanence in one context may emphasize transcendence in another. What the terms mean depends in part on the metaphysical assumptions, usually unconscious, of those who use them.

A distinction must be made between epistemological and ontological discussions. For some, the crucial question is whether God can be conceived and talked about in a more or less coherent way. Those who deny this call God "transcendent." The human mind, they believe, is capable of dealing with ordinary, mundane things but is not capable of understanding God. God is mystery, and that mystery is not like detective stories that call us to use our wits to solve the mystery or like the extremely puzzling questions that confront physicists. The God mystery is inherently and necessarily a mystery, a mystery before which we can only stand in awed silence.

Some of those who emphasize this epistemological transcendence believe, nevertheless, that God can be experienced through forms of mysticism. The experience is ineffable, but expressions that come from it point in some way to the mystery. Others believe

31

that the utterly mysterious God is revealed in particular events. For Christians, these are events recorded in the Bible, and especially the event of Jesus Christ.

Some emphasize the divine mystery without allowing for either mysticism or revelation as a bridge between creatures and God. This is the most extreme form of epistemological transcendence. David Hume pointed out that one can hardly distinguish this form of belief from atheism, since nothing intelligible is actually affirmed in asserting belief in such a God.

With respect to epistemological transcendence, process theology is strongly on the immanentalist side. Whitehead taught that God is not an exception to the metaphysical categories. God is an actual entity, as are all the creatures, so that God exemplifies all the features that pertain to actual entities as such. When we say that God loves us, we mean that real similarity exists between God's relation to us and the most ideal aspects of a mother's relation to her daughter.

Of course, God is very different from the creatures. All the other actual entities are actual occasions; that is, they have finite spatiotemporal locations. God does not. In important ways, God remains very mysterious. God's everlastingness and relatedness to all things boggle the mind. We are far from having a fully coherent doctrine of God's being and activity. The mind is also boggled by what we are learning of subatomic entities and of cosmic origins and by the relation of brains and personal experience, as well. It seems that the more we know, the more mysterious our world becomes. Still, this is not the kind of radical, impenetrable mystery that accompanies views of epistemological transcendence.

The denial of radical epistemological transcendence has implications for ontological transcendence as well. The affirmation of epistemological transcendence is usually connected with the idea that God's being and nature are of a wholly different order from that of creatures. I have already indicated that process thought is at an opposite pole in this respect. It seeks metaphysical categories that are applicable to both God and the actual occasions that constitute empty space, as well as all our human experiences.

Sometimes the meaning of immanent is more spatial than qualitative. Is God to be found inside nature or inside human experience in contrast to outside? If one supposes that the world is made up of substantial things, each of which occupies a distinct space, then that question has a quite straightforward meaning. The idea that God is immanent then means that God is an element in the constitution of some or all of these substantial things. For example, God may be identified with the true self of every person, so that by going beneath the superficial flow of experience one may find God.

It is hard to see how pure immanence can be affirmed, even in this case. If God is the true self of every person, then God as a whole seems vastly to transcend each individual person, even if God is to be found within each. The alternative would be a vast plurality of gods, one in each person, which would make the use of the word "God" extremely problematic. In fact, this doctrine as historically developed in India leads to the identification of the true self, atman, with the ground of all being, Brahman, and Brahman is in many ways transcendent. Nevertheless, the movement toward God, when understood in this way, may be purely immanent.

When transcendence is affirmed in this spatial sense, God becomes very remote. If God is not present in the creatures, and the creatures jointly occupy all space, then God is outside of space. What we call "Deism" often pictured God in this way, as outside the universe, acting on it from without or simply leaving it alone. It has become extremely difficult to reconcile such a vision with the picture of the universe emerging from ongoing developments in science. Nevertheless, much Christian language suggests that God acts on creatures from outside them. Sometimes this is the meaning of "transcendence." In this sense, process thought rejects "transcendence."

What it means to be immanent or transcendent changes when one thinks, with process thought, of the world as made up of events or occasions of experience. These are largely constituted by their relations to past events or occasions of experience. These relations are internal rather than external, in the sense that the relations participate in constituting the occasions of experience. Whitehead's most original contribution, the idea of "prehension," explains how what is external becomes internal, or how that which is spatiotemporally transcendent becomes immanent.

Do we then seek God within, or without? The answer is both-and and neither-nor, because the language of external and internal comes from a metaphysics that process thought rejects. God is a truly constitutive part of our experience, moment by moment, but the God who is constitutive of our experience is present in this way throughout the universe, drastically transcending us.

Process theologians see this relationship as one that the church tried to express in its idea of incarnation and in the way the Holy Spirit works within us. The God who was incarnate in Jesus radically transcended the finite Jesus but was truly constitutive of Jesus' being. The Holy Spirit that indwells believers is radically transcendent of believers but is truly immanent with them. In the process vision, nothing about this is especially mysterious. Everything that is immanent is transcendent, and everything that is transcendent is immanent. Immanence and transcendence are mutually implicative.

Nevertheless, in relation to the teaching of divine transcendence in many churches, the unquestionable emphasis of process theology is that the transcendent God is immanent in every creature and especially in human experience. We think that both the gospels and the Pauline letters support this way of thinking. Jesus addressed God as Abba in a way that does not suggest divine remoteness or utter mystery. When Paul said that Christ is in us and we are in Christ, Christ cannot be only a transcendent being, that is, one implies the other.

We may seek God in our own quiet immediate experience. We may seek God in the stories of the Bible and especially in Jesus. We may seek God in the ongoing life of the church. We may seek God in cosmic evolution. We may even try to imagine what it is like to be God. However we approach God, it is the same God, both immanent and transcendent, whom we approach.

Is it correct to think of God as the dominant occasion in the universe?

Before offering answers to the remaining questions about God, I feel the need for a word of caution. The first and surest answer is that neither I, nor Hartshorne, nor Whitehead, nor anyone else has ever known the answers to questions of this sort. In a strict sense of "know," this lack of knowledge applies to most of the questions I try to answer, but questions that press for the exact nature of God and God's relation to the world, especially from God's side, require this disclaimer more than others. Whitehead made such a disclaimer before beginning his religiously most interesting discussion near the end of *Process and Reality*. His disciples should not forget to repeat it.

Nevertheless, it is good and proper that we try to shape our imaging of God in the most reasonable and plausible way we can. Those of us who find process thought the most reasonable and plausible way of understanding ourselves and our world try to use it also to think about God. At that point, even the limited sort of testing that is possible with our ideas about ourselves and our world eludes us. But we do not cease, for that reason, to think. What models, derivative from our theories about the world, work best when we are thinking of God?

The questioner asks about the model of the "dominant occasion." That idea was developed by Whitehead to depict the occasion of human experience in its relation to the other occasions that make up the human organism. It works for other animals as well, at least the vertebrate ones with brains. It points to the fact that although there are many centers of life and activity in the body, by far the most influential one is located somewhere in the brain. Its decisions have far greater importance in determining the behavior of the whole organism than do those of any other entity in the body. The dominant occasion is also called the "final percipient occasion," because the body is organized to channel stimulation from sources both in and outside the body, through the central nervous system, to the brain. The final percipient occasion plays a dominant role because it is informed of so much.

At the same time, it is important to emphasize that as richly as this occasion is informed, its continuing ignorance far outweighs its knowledge of what goes on either in its body or in its environment. The information it receives and processes is very limited, indeed. Similarly, although it is the most influential occasion in the body, its "dominance" is only very partial. In most cases it has little influence on the heart, for example. During sleep, its dominance is greatly reduced. Even in the areas where it has the strongest influence, the dominant occasion depends on the good functioning of the brain and that depends on the good functioning of other parts of the body. For example, I am now typing on my computer, and my fingers follow my thoughts quite well. But damage to some of the nerves would quickly end that influence. The influence is less vulnerable in relation to spatially proximate neuronal events in the brain.

So how effective is this dominant occasion model for explaining the relationship of God with the world? We can compare it with some others that have been used–for example, a king and his subjects. In this comparison, the model of dominant occasion is better. The relation of dominant occasion better expresses the intimacy and mutuality of the relationship. Also, the dominant occasion works only internally on its adjacent occasions. We also know that what happens to the body deeply affects the dominant occasion, and we believe that whatever happens in the world affects God.

The king may work partly by persuading subjects, but the relationship is largely mediated through laws. There is always the threat of externally imposed punishment. Also, the king may be unaffected by what happens to many of his subjects. On the other hand, the king's subjects are more obviously free agents able to resist the demands of the king than are bodily cells, so the monarchical model has some advantages. A better one, especially for Christians, would be parent and child. Nevertheless, if these are our choices, I vote for the dominant occasion.

What we mean by a dominant occasion, or better, by a series of dominant occasions, is what the Greeks meant by "psyche." Some of the Greek philosophers speculated that the relationship of God to the world was like that of psyche to soma. That may have worked better for them than it does for us. They tended more to think of the psyche as the enlivening force of the whole body. God is surely spatially related to every part of the universe equally. We locate the dominant occasion more fully in the brain and often at a particular place within the brain. This means that it is related directly to only a few loci in the brain, and to every other part of the body indirectly. That analogy is not good. But even the Greeks had limitations. The psyche might be coterminous with the soma, but it still had a spatially external relation to most of reality. The psyche's relations to the wider environment played a large role in shaping the psyche, whereas God has no spatially external environment. Still, if the model simply says that the relation of God to the world is like that of the psyche to the soma, understanding the psyche as pervading the soma is a good place to start.

This explanation of God's relation to the world is much more an analogy than a model. A model may be thought of as an abstract pattern that is literally exemplified in more than one kind of thing. An analogy normally has some similarities and some dissimilarities to its referent. In some respects God is related to the world as soul is related to body. In other respects, important ones, the relation is quite different. Hartshorne liked the analogy. Whitehead never mentioned it, as far as I am aware. I personally have used the analogy of soul to brain to avoid, or at least reduce, the problem of spatial separation and mediation of influence.

If we think of the soul as more or less coterminous with the brain, influenced by what happens in the brain and also influencing it, the analogy is one with which we can begin to think of God and the world. This analogy also helps to explain why we should not expect to understand God very well. An enormous difference exists between the subjective life of an individual neuron and a unified human experience. Presumably the difference between a momentary human experience and that of God is even greater. We can speculate that the relation is similar in that God includes our experiences and unifies them, somewhat as we include the experiences of the neurons and unify them. We can also speculate that God includes our experiences perfectly as well as those of the neurons. Our inclusion of neuronal experience is very imperfect, and our inclusion of the quantum events of which these neuronal experiences are ultimately composed is even vaguer. That God includes and unifies the whole world is a very bold claim and certainly not one implicit in the analogy. Still I think it more reasonable to make that claim than to press the analogy too far.

The other part of the question points to one reason that Hartshorne used the analogy and Whitehead did not. Hartshorne thought that the divine life consists in a series of divine occasions, just as the human soul consists in such a series. Hence, one can ground the analogy in a momentary occasion on both sides. Indeed, one reason Hartshorne thinks of God in this manner is so that more of the ways of understanding ourselves and our world can be understood to be applicable to God as well.

For example, in the world, an occasion can only function as a cause of what transpires in another occasion when it has become complete. At that point it ceases to be a subject and becomes an object for others. Process thought understands God to influence what happens in all occasions. That seems to require that God's process of becoming becomes complete and thus available as an object to be felt by others. When I wrote *A Christian Natural Theology* (1965), I was influenced by that line of reasoning. In the second edition (2007), I revised my formulations. Many process theologians continue to follow Hartshorne on this point.

Whitehead, however, never adopted this view. He held that God is an "actual entity" but not an "actual occasion." God's relation to time, he thought, is not like ours. God and the world are complementary to each other. God is not another example of worldly occasions. This understanding created some tension with his other famous statement, that God is the supreme exemplification of the categories, not an exception. Hartshorne followed the implication of that statement better than Whitehead. However, I have come gradually to prefer Whitehead's emphasis on complementarity to Hartshorne's emphasis on metaphysical similarity. Again, we are far beyond the reliable limits of human thought and have no empirical check for either view.

Hartshorne's view of God as a serially ordered succession of divine experiences does not require special explanation. It provides a positive answer to the first question and supports a positive answer to the second. I fully respect this view. It has its problems, but I am convinced that we run into problems when we press any question very far, whether about God or the world or ourselves. I think we can press them further, with fewer problems, through a process conceptuality than through any other I know. But even with the process view, we still face plenty of problems.

The problem with thinking of God as one everlasting concrescence, as Whitehead did, strikes one immediately. The whole reason for bringing up the topic of God in the first place is because God makes a difference in the world. Yet in Whitehead's conceptuality, to make a difference is to be prehended, and an actual entity cannot be prehended during its concrescence. I have too much respect for Whitehead to think that he simply made a conceptual blunder here, so I was pleased when Marjorie Suchocki, reading the texts carefully, came up with a clue to Whitehead's thinking.

Actual occasions in the world have no unity until they have unified their many data. They originate physically and achieve their unification conceptually. Until they have become "one," they do not exist for others. God is different. God is a unity of conceptual feelings primordially, or eternally. All possibility is unified in God in such a way that its relevance to what is to be actual is established. That unity is complete and, therefore, can be prehended. It is this completed unity whose effectiveness in the world is the primary topic of Whitehead's philosophical writings so far as God is concerned. Without this completed unity there could be neither order nor novelty; indeed, there could be nothing at all.

In the world, conceptual feelings are added to the physical ones and are required to unify them. Only as conceptual feelings bring unity to the whole occasion do they achieve their own unity. But God begins in conceptual unity. God's physical feelings of the world are woven upon the always already-unified conceptual feelings. Hence they ipso facto become part of that unity. God's satisfaction grows with these additions, but this growth is not episodic.

One reason for the difference between Hartshorne and White-head on this topic is that they have different views of forms, or what Whitehead calls "eternal" objects. "Eternal," like "primordial," means nontemporal. It is not an honorific term. Eternal objects are pure possibilities. Whether there will ever be a universe in which eternal objects might become really possible is a different question that makes no difference to what they are in their absolute abstractness. Even in their absolute abstractness, they are related to one another, and how they are related to one another also determines how they are related to a world in which some of them are ingredient. The relatedness among them provides order and novelty to the world. This sphere of ordered possibility constitutes the being of God eternally. No analogy exists among creatures. The being of God eternally is the presupposition of creaturely existence.

So far as I can tell, Hartshorne is not interested in this level of abstraction. The possibilities in which he is interested are the real possibilities for this world. For him, new possibilities are coming into being. Creatures create them. To him it seems that if all symphonies already exist as possibilities in God, real creaturely creativity is belittled. What Whitehead called the primordial nature plays no role in Hartshorne's thought. Hence, the only thing that is eternal is the essence of God. That essence can be fully actualized in every occasion of the divine life. To think of the primordial nature of God being recreated in every moment is more awkward.

Although I began with Hartshorne's view, I have come to find Whitehead's vision of God more profound and, therefore, for me, more credible and more satisfying. That is simply a confession, not an argument. In any case, I assume that the reality is far beyond these human concepts and the limits of our imagination.

What is a very simple definition of the concept of "aims," as in "God's aims" for me or us?

What are God's aims? The questioner is not asking what God's aims for us are in their specificity, but rather what we mean when we say that God has aims for us. It is a good question, and quite central for the practical meaning of process theology. I'll try to explain as simply and clearly as I can.

In *Religion in the Making,* Whitehead referred several times to an experience that he believes is widespread. We sense the existence of a rightness that is objective to our preferences. Some ways of being and acting are genuinely better than others. This rightness cannot be reduced to our preferences or our calculation of what is best for us as individuals. Traditional philosophies and religions explain this in different ways. Traditional philosophies and religions all take for granted that some ways of being and acting are truly better than others.

One may, of course, explain this as social conditioning. A tribe would not survive if its children were not socialized to act in ways that helped it do so. Socialization shapes the sense of what is right in diverse ways. Perhaps no further explanation is needed.

However, Whitehead thought that this experience involves more than the effects of socialization. Individuals have a sense of rightness that can be in tension with their social conditioning. We are likely to judge that, generally speaking, the mores of our group reflect objective rightness and express it adequately enough to be our guide. Our ability to distinguish what is truly right from what the community expects of us indicates that our sense of rightness is not exhausted by our conditioning.

Whitehead was especially interested in the insights attained by reflective members of what he calls the "rational religions." These are the major traditional religious movements arising in several parts of the world around 2,500 years ago in which individual experience and conviction became decisively important. These traditions, such as Judaism and its offspring, Christianity and Islam, philosophical Hinduism, Buddhism, Taoism, Confucianism, and Zoroastrianism, all emphasize a rightness that transcends social mores.

In *Religion in the Making,* Whitehead emphasized that this intuition of rightness gives no direct evidence for a personal God. Buddhism stresses the dharmas, Confucianism speaks of li, Taoism of the tao, and so forth, without positing a deity in the Judaic sense. Yet a theistic explanation is also plausible, and Whitehead in fact opted for it.

The Abrahamic faiths tend to speak of divine laws, and even the nontheistic accounts of rightness normally explain this experience in terms of static principles. Whitehead was not satisfied with that. What people experience is not unchanging rules of conduct but a much more specific and localized rightness. Indeed, loyalty to the felt rightness may be in tension with following principles that have been laid down in the past based on the same type of intuitions. Whitehead believed this could most accurately be explained if we understood that each momentary experience has an objective best. The occasion of experience must constitute itself somehow out of the past world that flows into it. Some ways of doing this are really better than others. Theistic believers understand themselves to be called by God to actualize themselves in those better ways.

Whitehead occasionally spoke of the "best." He recognized that some circumstances offer no good choices–that the "best" is only the least bad. Usually this notion of a best makes sense. Sometimes, more than one decision may be equally good. Indeed, it is often more important to decide matters quickly than to concern ourselves with discerning which of two more or less equal decisions is best. God's call may be precisely to decide quickly.

Another qualification is important if we are to understand Whitehead. We make many choices over which we deliberate consciously for shorter or lengthier times. We decide which college to attend, what dress to wear, or how to respond to an offensive letter. Of course, for Whitehead, these are decisions, and it is important to choose well. Whitehead focused on the decisions made moment by moment. These moments contain no possibility of laying out pros and cons and weighing them against each other. The response to the received data is spontaneous rather than reflective. Of course, the best spontaneous response may be to decide to pause and reflect, but such is the rare, not the normal, response. In any case, the decision about which college to attend finally results from innumerable smaller decisions about what catalogs to read and with whom to talk and how attentively to listen.

Some people suppose that what happens in a moment of their experience cannot be considered a "decision" at all. From a Whiteheadian perspective, if there is no decision moment by moment, then the term "decision" will not be useful in the larger context either. The reality will be that all is always fully determined by what is given.

As an example that may help to understand what is meant, consider a driver confronted by a sudden change, perhaps a reckless driver cutting in. We often say that it is important to have good reflexes. If all that is required to avoid an accident is applying the brakes, the idea of reflexes may suffice. Suppose that someone is tailgating so that abrupt slowing would be very dangerous. Perhaps the best alternative is to swerve quickly into another lane while increasing speed. That will not be a reflex in any simply sense.

Later, when the driver explains why she swerved into another lane, she can lay out her options and show that this was the best. The moment does not allow for any verbal consideration of the options. In a fraction of a second, one sees the situation and decides what to do. Decisions do occur in the moment. Of course, most of them are far less dramatic.

Whitehead approached questions of this sort not only through an account of human experience but also cosmologically. That is, he considered the status in reality of what is widely intuited by reflective people. Where are the possibilities located among which a choice is made?

Most philosophers have thought that what happens in any event is the outcome of what has happened in antecedent events. This approach allows for no decisions. If the philosophers are theists, they may include the divine reality as one of the causal forces or even as the all-determining one. Whitehead believed that the intuition that we are partly responsible for what we do and become invalidates this widespread belief. To be responsible means that we are not entirely determined by what is given to us, whether creaturely or divine. This means that we are partly self-determining. Each momentary human occasion makes a decision about itself, about just how it will constitute itself from what is given to it.

An occasion cannot choose what will be given to it. In Whitehead's view, the occasion will be physically shaped by the occasions in its past as they flow into it. There is no responsibility there. The occasion feels, or "prehends" possibilities as well as actualities. If only one set of possibilities could actually be realized given the physical world of that moment, then this would only add another causal determinant. But Whitehead argued that alternative possibilities are felt and that the occasion has to decide among them.

This picture introduces God. Prehensions of possibilities do not normally constitute an awareness of feeling God, but Whitehead believed that possibilities cannot simply present themselves. Indeed, to have any reality or effectiveness at all, they must be in an actuality. To have any relevance to the situation, they must be ordered. Whitehead called the locus of these ordered possibilities "God."

The intuition of a rightness in the world is not satisfied simply by the existence of alternative relevant possibilities rendered effective for the occasion. This intuition of a rightness requires that alternative relevant possibilities be valued *for* the occasion and not only *by* the occasion. This leads to the idea that God offers these alternative possibilities to us with some gradation of valuation. Some of them are better than others. God calls us toward the better without in any way preventing us from choosing the worse.

Whitehead's technical term for this valuing of some relevant possibility as best for the occasion was "initial aim," or more elaborately, the "initial stage of the subjective aim." What Whitehead called the "initial aim" corresponds to the questioner's language of "God's aims for us." The initial phase of an occasion is the inflow into it of the world and God. The inflow of the world may favor the actualization of possibilities that are real but less than ideal. In this case, the final form of the subjective aim, the one that determines just what decision will be made, is likely to fall short of the initial (God's) aim. But the feeling of the ideal possibility will not be wholly lost. It will linger as a sense of missed opportunity. In New Testament language, there will be a sense of hamartia. This is typically translated "sin," but it more accurately means "missing the mark." This sense of missing the mark is testimony to the sense that there is a mark–an ideal possibility or aim from God–that has been missed.

Is God's "aim" similar to God's "call"?

This question asks how to relate Whitehead's technical doctrine of the initial subjective aim to the biblical idea of God's calling. This is important in itself and also as illustrative of the task of this kind of philosophical theology. I like the term "calling" and so use it often in describing how God deals with us. As far as I know, Whitehead did not use this word.

Whitehead believed that in every moment our experience is characterized by purposiveness. This does not mean that we always act with a clear, conscious intention. But everything we do expresses in some way our aim to continue living, to live well, and to live better. In each situation, this aim has a particular content relevant to the concrete situation in which we find ourselves. The aim may be to go back to sleep, to protect oneself from the cold, to get something to eat, to help a friend, to become more responsive to God. Most of these aims are rooted in one's bodily conditions, but they are not simply physical. They depend on taking into account some sense of unrealized possibility contrasted with what is. For example, if one is trying to satisfy one's thirst, what is at work is not simply the physical discomfort but the awareness of an alternative possibility and attraction toward it.

This awareness of and desire for an alternative preferred possibility is the "subjective aim" of the occasion. The aim is derived from what Whitehead called the "primordial" ordering of possibilities that establishes the relevance of these possibilities to every concrete situation. Every momentary experience arises largely out of its past and its body, but it also arises out of the "prehension," or feeling, of relevant possibilities. Whitehead termed these possibilities "lures." The experience of these lures constitutes the initial phase of the subjective aim. As the occasion integrates these possibilities with the actualities inherited from the past, the subjective aim develops for good or ill.

It is not, I think, hard to sense that our actions are purposeful even when we are not conscious of the purpose. For the most part our purposes are not conscious, certainly not clearly so. In this respect, the examples I have given and the language in which I describe them may be misleading. Whitehead thought that consciousness illumines only the more complex features of our experience, whereas the aim, especially in its initial phase, is quite simple.

The initial phase of the subjective aim is derived from God's ordering of possibility. It is the best possibility for that situation. It aims at realizing value in the occasion itself and also through its impact on future occasions. It does not compel the occasion to realize that possibility in its fullness. Also, it does not dictate just how it will change as these abstract possibilities are integrated with the conditions provided by the past. The occasion may fall short of the ideal possibility for its actualization. Indeed, this often seems to occur, at least with human beings.

A gap separates what Christians commonly mean by God's "calling" them and this philosophical account. Nevertheless, a congeniality joins them. The idea of God's call is that God leads us to feel that a particular decision is the right one for us. In Protestant circles the idea of calling has sometimes been tied especially to the decision to enter the ministry. The Reformers emphasized that every form of socially useful work can also be regarded as a calling. The wide use of the word "vocation" still today expresses that sense. In the Bible, Jesus calls people to follow him and God calls people to prophesy. It is not unusual for Christians to say they feel called to help someone or to contribute to some cause. I would like to extend the use of the term still further, and I am far from alone in this. I believe that God calls us moment by moment to be what it is possible, in that moment, to be. This comes close to Whitehead's account.

The biblical stories of God's calling show that a call may be resisted or even refused. Not all who are called respond. Nevertheless, the call is important for all. Failure to respond does not mean that God's calling ceases. This also comes close to Whitehead's account. The calling by God makes possible actions that would not otherwise be possible. It does not determine that they will be taken.

For process theologians, the choice of how widely or how narrowly to use a word like "God's call" is an open question. Certainly we will use it most often when we refer to major, fully conscious decisions. For us, these occasional and important decisions are usually a product of many, many smaller decisions. We do not see God's calling as an abrupt introduction of a relation that is otherwise wholly absent. We see, rather, that God is continuously drawing us toward increased sensitivity, increased willingness to take risks, and increased caring for others, and it is only as we have often allowed ourselves to be drawn in these directions that we can receive and respond to the dramatic callings on which we usually focus. Because I see continuity between the many small, mainly unconscious, decisions and the occasional major conscious ones, I prefer to use the same terminology throughout. I think of the initial aim derived from God as God's continual calling of all of us, Christians and others, to be and to do the best that is possible in each situation.

I think of God's calling of us in each moment as God's wholly free gift to us. It is God's grace. When we refuse and resist, God's grace can also become God's judgment, but it is always a gracious judgment. God does not give up on us. What was possible before one became addicted to cocaine is no longer possible. Still, possibilities may open up to seek help to overcome the addiction. Even if one succeeds in overcoming addiction, one must still accept the fact that much that would have been possible had one not succumbed to the temptation is now forever impossible. A recovering addict can discover new possibilities that renew the path of growth. God offers us what we can receive.

I also think of God's calling in each moment as guidance and providence. By offering us the best possibility for that moment, God is giving us genuine and realistic guidance. The more sensitive and responsive we become, the more fully we will be guided. Divine providence works this way in the world.

I stated that this discussion of the initial aim and calling can serve as a model for the movement from philosophical conceptuality to Christian language. In this case, the philosophy frees us to use the theological language more straightforwardly than many modern people think possible. If the only way one can imagine being called by God is to hear a voice from heaven, then one may well regard this concept as having little applicability or even none at all. If one refers instead to a deep inward awareness of better and worse ways of constituting ourselves, many people can find resonance.

Those who oppose this way of relating philosophy and theology sometimes do so because they suppose that all the biblical language is bound up with supernaturalism. I believe that this reading of the Bible imposes upon it a later framework. This later framework juxtaposes a self-sufficient nature to the realm of God. Hence God can only act on the world from outside it and can only do so in a way that violates the integrity of nature. Nothing like this appears in the Bible itself. The Bible knows no self-sufficient nature. God is a factor in what happens in the world. In some instances God works in ways that are radically unexpected. Because there is no self-sufficient nature with its established laws, there is also no supernatural intervention.

Differences exist between the worldviews underlying the Bible and the one that emerges from Whitehead's reflections. Nevertheless, given the difference in time and context, the similarities are more surprising than the differences. Whitehead advocated no supernaturalism because nature does not exist apart from God's creative involvement. God's working in the world is internal to actual experience. That does not make it less real or less important. Given this vision, the notion of God intervening or setting aside the laws of nature simply makes no sense. God calls, directs, and transforms from within. As far as my experience goes, this is the kind of calling, directing, and transforming for which most thoughtful Christians hope.

What does it mean to say that God includes such things as genocide, rape, and murder in both the primordial nature and the consequent nature? How then can God be good?

Since God includes all pure potentials or possibilities (eternal objects) in the primordial nature and all that happens in the world in the consequent nature, there is certainly an important sense in which God includes the evil along with the good. Nevertheless, process theologians argue that God is perfectly good. How is this possible?

With regard to what is eternally included in the primordial nature of God, genocide, rape, and torture are not good examples. I incline to say that they are not eternal objects at all. Let me explain.

The eternal objects and their ordering, Whitehead said, presuppose that there will be some actual world, but they do not presuppose any contingent particularities about that actual world. The only ideas I have that in any way correspond with genocide, rape, and torture presuppose the actuality of human beings. One might argue that a cat sometimes "tortures" a mouse, so I will not strictly insist on that limitation. Without living beings, at least, there can be no torture. All three terms refer primarily to what human beings sometimes do to one another.

For Whitehead, our ideas of such things are "propositions" or "impure possibilities." In ordinary language, most of our references to possibilities are to this type. We are thinking of what is possible in a given situation or for given people. The realm of eternal objects makes no reference to any actual situation or people. Possibilities of this impure sort, that is, what Whitehead called "propositions," emphatically come into being progressively in the course of evolution and history. They are not included in God's primordial nature.

Does this mean that there are no "evil" eternal objects? I'm not sure how to answer that, but at least the question can lead to a deeper probe. Two species of eternal objects exist: objective and subjective. Those entities typically considered by mathematicians, such as shapes and quantities, are of the objective species. That is, one can think of them and about them, but one cannot characterize the subjective form of the experience in which such thought occurs. It is safe to say that eternal objects of the objective species are neither good nor bad, although the ingression of a particular shape into a particular painting may be aesthetically good or bad.

With respect to eternal objects of the subjective species, matters are not quite that simple, and I am less sure of my answer. These eternal objects are qualities of feeling. A particular sense of aesthetic pleasure is an eternal object of this species. It remains an object about which thought is possible, but it can also characterize human subjectivity. The same is true of a particular form of pain.

Are, then, the eternal objects–pain and suffering–evil? For God to feel every possible form of pain and suffering subjectively would seem evil. My understanding, however, is that God feels such pain and suffering subjectively only in God's sympathetic feeling of the feelings of creatures who feel them. God's primordial envisagement of the eternal objects does not involve their ingression into the subjective form of the divine experience. In the primordial nature, even eternal objects of the subjective species are felt by God only objectively. If readers agree that we can communicate with one another about the ideas of pain and suffering without feeling them subjectively, then this should not be difficult to understand.

Would it have been better if the realm of pure possibility did not include pain and suffering at all? Pain has important positive roles as well as negative ones. Some suffering is an expression of love and seems ennobling. Surely few people would argue for their total exclusion. The focus of the examples of evil we have been considering is probably more on the malice of those who inflict pain and suffering than on the victims. Hence the more searching question is whether it would have been better for God to have excluded malice from the realm of pure possibility.

The question suggests a more voluntaristic view of God than I find in Whitehead. God's role in relation to the eternal objects is not, I think, to create them out of nothing or to decide whether they should exist but only to order them so as to encourage the emergence of increased value in the world. Even so, the question remains interesting. Would we choose to live in a world where willing harm to others was not only absent but also not conceivable or possible of realization? In such a world, would willing good for others be conceivable or possible of realization? Would there be any moral experience at all? Would this be an improvement?

These are not easy questions to answer. I am persuaded that the total value realized in a world where malice was not simply lacking but utterly inconceivable would be less than in one where people struggle with moral choices. We Whiteheadians generally think that progress in the realization of positive values inevitably involves increased possibilities for evil as well, so that God could not have ordered things so as to have rich experiences without pain and suffering. This assertion is highly speculative, and it is not directly derived from Whitehead's texts, although we think it is consistent with them.

My response to the concern about the inclusion of evil in God's primordial nature has been chiefly that what is included is far too abstract to be evil in itself. Evil arises through the ingression of certain eternal objects into certain actual occasions at certain times. That is, evil is to be found in actual entities, not the eternal objects. This emphasis in no way reduces the concerns expressed in the second part of the question. What about the consequent nature, in which the immediacy of feeling to be found in every occasion is forever preserved? Does not that introduce evil into God?

In Whitehead's view it certainly introduces suffering into God. Much of that suffering is unnecessary. Creatures could have made different choices that would have reduced the suffering in the world and therefore also in God.

Traditional theology resisted the idea that God is capable of suffering. God's perfection meant that God was free of suffering. Patripassianism was condemned as a heresy. The idea that God suffers with us, however, is not alien to the Bible. I am not sure that the questioner is bothered by this way in which evil is in God.

The problem, again, may be more with the inclusion of the maliciousness of the perpetrator of suffering. The experience of the Marquis de Sade, taking pleasure in the agony of children, is preserved forever in God. Perhaps this is what distresses the questioner. It seems to have troubled Whitehead also, since he qualified his general statement a little in response.

I will not, however, try to exegete the qualifications. Instead, let us consider the basic question of the vivid memory of evil. What alternatives should we consider? For Jews, no memory can be more horrible than that of the Shoah, or Holocaust. No doubt some Jews want to forget it. For most Jews, despite the pain that is reenacted in its memory, it is important that its memory remain vivid.

The horror of this event makes it more difficult for Jews to reconcile their belief in God as Lord of History with the actual course of events. On the whole they do not regard this as a reason for minimizing the event. It belongs to the reality of Jewish history, and apart from it that history is not adequately incorporated.

The situation is similar in the case of individuals. Some women deal with rape by blocking out the memory. To recall it is too painful. However, in the majority of cases, this strategy of denial generates more problems than it resolves. For most, the path of healing leads through the renewal of memory and its incorporation into one's life story.

These are only analogies, of course, and analogies should not be pressed. Nevertheless, if we think of the universe story as God's story, we may be able to see that selective memory would not suffice. The story needs to include everything, however painful this may be to God.

Perhaps the questioner fears that if God contains the malicious feelings of the torturer, God's own motives will be tainted. This would misrepresent the way in which God contains the world. Again analogy may help. A good parent empathizes deeply with the feelings of children. Empathy is a way of including the feelings of the other. Perhaps the child is angry at a playmate, and the parent feels the child's anger. Still the parent feels the anger as the child's anger.

Empathy does not involve the parent's becoming angry with the playmate. Ideally, the parent can at the same time be empathetic with the playmate. The emotional resources of the child probably do not allow for both anger and empathy toward the playmate, but children can grow into adults for whom this greater complexity of feeling, however difficult, does become possible. What is just possible to some small extent in mature human beings, Whitehead posited as ideally fulfilled in God. The inclusion of evil in God belongs to God's goodness.

How do you answer the criticism that the God of process theology is "weak"?

This month I am writing in response to comments by John Polkinghorne in an interview by Michael Fitzgerald published in the January 29, 2008, issue of *Christian Century*. Polkinghorne is a theologian who was once a physicist and does theology with physics constantly in view. This makes his work quite parallel to process theology. But Polkinghorne takes the occasion to criticize process theology, claiming that "its God is too weak." Polkinghorne resonates with the "the fellow sufferer" described by Whitehead, but finds this God, overall, could not have raised Jesus from the dead. Since I think his criticism is rather widely shared, I will discuss it.

Although he does not reject the "fellow sufferer," Polkinghorne's emphasis lies on God's active power in making things happen. The resurrection of Jesus is the central image of this power, and although Polkinghorne does not explain just how he understands that, it is in a sense that he thinks process theologians cannot affirm. God must be able to redeem suffering through some great fulfillment–also presumably in a sense that process theology cannot affirm.

The form of process theology that follows Whitehead has a well-worked-out way for understanding how God acts in the world. It fits fairly well with the image of God acting more as an orchestra conductor, evoking responses, than as a puppet master, pulling strings. Some process theologians have used the image of the orchestra conductor, although I think it limits the role of the players a bit too much. It understands God's role in the resurrection of Jesus as metaphysically the same as God's role in other events. Of course, process theology emphasizes that God is the reason for novelty in the world and that God is always doing something new. Polkinghorne seems to want something different. He seems to want to say that God's mode of acting in the resurrection was different from God's mode of acting before and that this new mode of acting gives promise of the "great fulfillment."

Since Polkinghorne does not explain either how God works in general or how God worked in the resurrection, it is difficult for a process theologian to respond. Polkinghorne seems to want God's acts in miracles, which he goes on to discuss, not to destroy the congruence of theology and the established scientific worldview. However, he does not explain just how this is possible. For process theologians, it does not suffice to indicate that one believes there are miracles that are exceptions to the way God usually works but still do not conflict with what science teaches. Such beliefs need to be explained in a way that makes them credible.

However, my purpose here is not to criticize Polkinghorne, especially not on the basis of a single interview. My purpose is to take his criticism seriously as a religious statement. Process theology says a lot about God and about how God works in the world. Because of its understanding of the world, process theology can make sense of a good many traditional affirmations of Christianity that do not fit well into the dominant thought patterns of the secular world. For example, it can explain the role that faith can play in physical healings and even show the possibility of some other forms of miracle. Unlike most philosophies, it does not exclude the possibility of personal life beyond the death of the body. It shows that the often-reported appearance to loved ones of one who has died can be taken seriously. It certainly affirms the role of God in all of this.

I am not sure whether Polkinghorne understands the flexibility and openness of Whitehead's conceptuality in these respects. Yet I suspect that even if he did, he would still not be satisfied. The more intelligible and credible the stories become of miracles in general, and the resurrection specifically, the less they are seen as radically unique occurrences. For some Christians it is precisely their radical uniqueness that is crucial. I sense that this is true for Polkinghorne.

We confront here a real divide in the understanding of Christian faith. For process theology, Christianity is one religious movement among others. Some of us, standing in this movement, regard the wisdom and spiritual meaning it offers us as crucial for our lives. We find that it also opens us to the wisdom of other traditions, religious and secular. We can center our lives in Jesus Christ without denying the basic claims of other religious communities. We find that participating in Jesus' faithfulness is healing or saving for us and that in so doing we contribute to the healing and salvation of the world. For us, this is enough.

For others, and I gather these include Polkinghorne, the event that is at the heart of Christianity is not merely unique but belongs to a unique order of events, perhaps as its only member. For them, to fail to believe this is to miss the distinctiveness of Christian faith. This is partly because Christian faith involves confidence in an eventual "great fulfillment." Presumably this fulfillment can only occur in an event in which God acts in a way that is discontinuous from the way God ordinarily acts. In process language, the great fulfillment can come only in an event that is unilaterally caused by God. Thus Christology and eschatology belong together and fall outside the sphere that an enriched naturalism, such as process theology offers, can grasp.

My judgment is that a God who always participates with other entities in the coming into being of new events is *not* "too weak." Such a God is not too weak for the kind of Christian faithfulness process theology evokes. Such a God is "too weak" to bring about radically discontinuous events. That means that for those for whom Christian faith is the basis of the assurance of a final future outcome of history in which all is made right, process theology does not suffice. Process theologians do not exclude wonderful possibilities for the future, but we find little evidence that such expectations will be realized. We are not optimists about the course of history. We have *hope,* based on the inexhaustible wealth of possibilities with which God confronts the world, that the outcome of temporal events will indeed be profoundly fulfilling, but our faithfulness to Jesus Christ does not depend on that. We *do* believe that God empathizes with all that we are and do and will take all our existence and our actions up forever into the divine life. We long for a positive outcome of history. We are assured of a positive outcome in God. God has that power, and we consider it a very great power indeed.

This piece is not intended as an argument or a debate. For some contemporary Christians, including Polkinghorne, God's power includes the power to make creaturely events occur in just the way God and these believers desire. To believe that God has such a power can provide assurance that in fact the desired outcome will occur. This requires "faith" in the sense of believing that for which there is little evidence. From this point of view, a God who cannot ultimately effect whatever God wants is too weak. They are correct that, by this definition of strength, the God we process theologians affirm is weak.

To me, on the other hand, God does not seem weak at all. By virtue of God's power we live and think and hope and love. I believe we have good reasons for believing this, and I am deeply grateful for that power. I hope to use it to further life and thought and hope and love in others. I believe that is the faithful life to which I am called.

3

Whitehead and
the Process Tradition

Who is a Whiteheadian?

I have chosen this question because a good many people are influenced by Whitehead but tell me they are not Whiteheadians. Some of them give reasons that do not seem to me to have much to do with being, or not being, a Whiteheadian. I am not, of course, speaking of people who know Whitehead but basically reject his thought in favor of analytic philosophy or Kant or Spinoza. Clearly, these are right to say that they are not Whiteheadians even if they acknowledge some incidental influence. I am talking about people who do not turn to another philosophy but simply turn away from a focus on his.

Sometimes the issue is one of concerns and commitments. For example, one who has studied Whitehead with appreciation may be, or become, a liberation theologian, primarily concerned with overcoming oppression of one sort or another. He or she will then argue that one should draw on any source that helps in this task rather than being bound to a particular one.

Liberation from political and economic oppressions was not the focus of Whitehead's lifework. One needs to study and think about many topics to advance the cause of liberation, but one will not gain much on this subject from Whitehead's writings. For that purpose, the more useful writings would be historical, political, sociological, ethical, and theological. It may make some sense for someone to say I used to be a Whiteheadian, but now I am a liberation theologian, meaning that he or she once gave primary attention to Whitehead's writings and to promoting their study and now gives primary attention to another set of writings.

However, I resist this use of the term "Whiteheadian." In general, when one says one is a Platonist, an Aristotelian, or a Humean, one does not mean anything of this sort. One means only that on those issues that divide philosophers, one finds Plato, Aristotle, or Hume the most insightful and helpful thinker. One's primary interest may be business management, or poverty law, or understanding the psychodynamics of mental illness. One does not expect to study primarily the philosophers in question to advance one's knowledge.

The way I have made this point might suggest that philosophical commitments are irrelevant to thinking about the special topics. This is not the case. A Platonist is likely to formulate ideas about management somewhat differently from a Humean. An Aristotelian may be attentive to some features of the situation that the others do not notice. The point is only that among those with a common practical interest, followers of all three philosophers will be interested in much of the same literature and research. They will also be likely, because of their reading of current literature in many fields, to agree on some matters that are foreign to all their philosophical mentors.

Still they remain Platonist, Aristotelian, and Humean.

Sometimes what causes theologically oriented people who have been influenced by Whitehead to distance themselves from him is discomfort with the tenor and mood of his writings. For example, I often hear that someone cannot be a Whiteheadian because Whitehead was too optimistic. No doubt the cultural mood in the early twentieth century was more optimistic than the one that developed later. No doubt the tone of Whitehead's writings was affected by that cultural mood. Today we have solid reasons, based, for example, on ecological deterioration and global warming, to be profoundly pessimistic about the future of our planet. It would be foolish to look for anything like that in Whitehead's writings. I am deeply concerned about the future of the biosphere, and I do not read Whitehead to gain knowledge of this, but it does not occur to me for this reason to distance myself from Whitehead's conceptuality. Nothing in that conceptuality stands in tension with what we now know about human destruction of the environment. This does not mean that philosophy in general is neutral on this question. Hegel's philosophy is bound up with the view of a positive future. Dualistic philosophies such as Descartes's do not allow for the sort of interaction of human beings and the natural world that now play so large a role in the deterioration of the biosphere. Whitehead's conceptuality left the question of the health of the biosphere to the realm of empirical facts, allowing for human action that is either constructive or destructive. That human beings have chosen to continue pursuing a destructive course does not lead me to reject the conceptuality.

One might argue that, in fact, destructiveness has characterized human action for many millennia and that Whitehead failed to recognize this. This would be correct, in my opinion, on both counts. For example, he did not prepare his readers for the belated realization that for ten thousand years, agriculture has been eroding the soil. He underestimated the quality of life in hunting and gathering societies and overvalued civilization. Few people in his generation (very few, actually) saw these matters more clearly than did he. In many respects he was a child of his time and not in the lead in transcending them. If being a Whiteheadian meant taking him as my authority in all matters, I certainly could not be a Whiteheadian. So far as I can see, these limitations did not affect the basic pattern of his philosophical thought.

On more specifically theological matters, also, I do not follow Whitehead in some areas. He found little of value in the Hebrew Scriptures. His comments about Paul are quite negative. I belong to the form of Christianity that believes that the Hebrew Scriptures are extraordinarily rich and that appreciates Paul's theology deeply. So far as I can see, his judgments with which I disagree do not damage his contributions to thinking about God and about the relation of God and the world.

Although my commitment to Whitehead would remain even if I found him out of date and unhelpful on far more topics, I rejoice that he seemed to have been remarkably wise about many matters. Hence in addition to finding his basic conceptuality extraordinarily fruitful, I also relish the encounter with his wisdom, which is loosely related to that conceptuality. With respect to theology, I would follow much of his thinking about God even if he never mentioned Jesus or said foolish things about him. In fact I find his comments about Jesus as rich and inspiring today as when he wrote them many decades ago in a very different historical world.

A complex case has to do with sin. That is a theological concept, and Whitehead did not use it. Whitehead-influenced theologians sometimes feel they are departing from Whitehead when they write on this subject. My view is that, in fact, Whitehead's thought provided the basis for biblical and significant thinking about sin, although it certainly does not go far in this extremely complex field.

First, it makes the idea of "sin" meaningful. By this I mean that "sin" is meaningless if certain conditions do not obtain. To simplify, I will simply say that "sin" presupposes that better and worse are objectively distinguishable and are partially known as such by most people. Sin implies that despite all cultural relativities, "better" and "worse" are not simply functions of culture. Cultures are also shaped by perception of these differences. This objectivity must be related to God. This objectivity also implies that people have some control over their thoughts and their actions. Their thoughts and actions are not simply determined by past events. Sin has no reality unless people sometimes (actually, often and perhaps always) fail to act as well as they could. Whitehead's philosophy is extremely rare in providing all the needed elements for a doctrine of sin.

Second, Whitehead's thought favored some basic notions of sin over others. For example, it cut against notions of disobedience to divine rules or commandments. The God-world relation is not depicted rightly, in Whitehead's view, in terms of God as lawgiver and judge. Instead, God calls or lures creatures toward the best that is possible in concrete situations. People to some extent respond and to some extent resist. Many Christians judge that this is not the biblical understanding of sin. However, the most frequent word for "sin" in the New Testament is hamartia, which can be translated as "missing the mark." When Whitehead spoke of a rightness in things partly realized and partly missed, he seems to be talking about this "missing the mark."

The most interesting and religiously important contemporary discussion is about the many ways in which we miss the mark and how these are related to one another. It is about how deeply the tendency to miss the mark is rooted in our universal situation and how much depends on our particular communities and our individual experience. Contemporary discussion addresses how sin is related to repentance and forgiveness and about the possibility of transcending sin and, in some sense, becoming free of it. Modern theologians talk about how the work of Jesus plays into all of this. About such matters, Whitehead had very little to contribute. A Whiteheadian theologian will look to other sources than Whitehead for inspiration and guidance. One does not, for that reason, become less of a Whiteheadian.

In concluding, I will put matters in philosophical terms. Some philosophies imply that facts can be deduced from first principles. In these deterministic systems, metaphysics plays the controlling role. Whitehead emphatically rejected that type of philosophy. A central role for philosophy is to develop a metaphysics that makes clear the radical contingency of the world of facts.

The world of facts is also the world of values. Human attention should focus primarily on the world of facts and values. These can be studied empirically and historically. From empirical and historical study, theories can be developed, which then guide further study. These theories can then be tested in wider realms.

We can, of course, rest with theories that are successful in narrow fields but not coherently related to others. The modern university encourages this. Those who are satisfied with this narrow approach are truly not Whiteheadian. Whitehead encouraged the testing of theories by their coherence with other theories, seeking general theories that apply in multiple fields. The metaphysical goal is to find some very abstract theories that apply everywhere. Those who seek such sweeping generalizations and find more help in Whitehead's proposals than in others are Whiteheadians. So are those who work in particular fields in ways that build on or assume Whiteheadian ideas about reality. So are those who propose further development or refinements of his conceptuality, continuing the process that can be traced through his own writing.

I have written as if there were one correct way to use the term "Whiteheadian." Of course, that is itself misleading. People are free to define words as they choose. The question is whether, when detailed explanation does not accompany the term, the word will be understood. I have tried to stay close to what I judge to be a normal use of the term. I am writing against a tendency to understand it too restrictively.

No doubt I am doing so in part because some of these restrictive uses would seem to make being a Whiteheadian a very unattractive matter of slavishly agreeing with everything he said. Instead of liberating us to think in new and creative ways, as I have experienced it, Whitehead's philosophy would become a straightjacket imposed on those who accepted it. Few results would have been more distressing to Whitehead himself.

What is distinctive of Whitehead in relation to other process theologians?

This question reminds us that "process theologian" is a term that can refer to a wide range of thinkers. The recent publication of Gary Dorrien's third volume on the history of liberal theology in the United States reminds us of the central role that the Chicago school has played. It received extensive attention in Dorrien's second volume, dealing with the first half of the twentieth century, and it starts off the account of the subsequent history in the third volume. This volume also gives a full chapter to the Whiteheadian version of process theology.

The Chicago school named its theology in various ways. In the early part of the second half of the twentieth century, the most common label was "neonaturalism." The term "naturalism" juxtaposed it most emphatically to supernaturalism. Since the great majority of Christian teaching over the centuries has included supernaturalist elements, this contrast is of central importance. The Chicago school was committed to think theologically in a fully naturalistic way.

It shared this rejection of supernaturalism with many other Protestant theologians. Many of these followed Immanuel Kant, who is often called the philosopher of Protestantism. The term "naturalism" distinguishes the Chicago school from all those theologies that were informed by Kantian thought. These so emphasized the creativity of the human mind that the natural world was not seen as having any reality independent of human experience.

The term also distinguished it from Humean empiricism, since for that kind of empiricism, the only reality that could be attributed to nature was the sensa found in human experience. Naturalists believed that the natural world is far more extensive than the human one. Human existence is to be located within nature, but nature does not depend on human beings for its reality.

However, for many people the term "naturalism" suggested then, and still suggests, a reductionist, materialistic view. The Chicago thinkers were as concerned to reject materialism as idealism and sensationalist empiricism. They believed that new developments in science indicated that the world is not the clocklike machine that nature had often been taken for, at least since Descartes. They believed nature was far richer and more complex than that, so the inclusion of human beings within nature in no way implied that the human experience of freedom and responsibility, of love and commitment, was invalid.

This was a new naturalism and it depended on a new empiricism. William James spoke of a radical empiricism that understood experience, including the experience of the environment, as much richer and more complex than the sensationalist empiricists allowed. Thus the new naturalism and the radical empiricism supported one another in creating a context in which religious experience could be appreciatively studied.

The nature that emerged from this kind of thinking was always one in process. Human experience was one form of that process. History as a whole was an important expression of that process, so that some of the Chicago thinkers emphasized especially the social process. They did not accept the sort of dualism of history and nature that flourished in Kantian circles.

The word "process" appeared frequently in the writing of the Chicago school, but only Bernard Loomer lifted it up as a designation of this whole mode of thought. In doing so he was influenced by Whitehead, and especially by the title of Whitehead's magnum opus, *Process and Reality*. He and other Chicago thinkers recognized Whitehead as sharing with them all the points that I have listed earlier. He, too, was a neonaturalist. Indeed, Loomer clearly intended the term "process theology" to apply to the theological work of the Chicago school as a whole, including Whitehead. I use it in this way.

Nevertheless, the feelings toward Whitehead among leaders of the Chicago school were ambivalent. On the one hand, they recognized their kinship and knew they were dealing with a towering figure in science, mathematics, and philosophy. On the other hand, they were uncomfortable both with his speculative method and also with the conclusions to which it led him, especially with respect to God. Henry Nelson Wieman at first interpreted Whitehead in a favorable light but eventually rejected his thought harshly. Bernard Meland always kept his distance, treating Whitehead on a par with many other thinkers from whose thought one could draw useful ideas without in any way committing to his systematic work. Bernard Loomer was drawn deeply into Whitehead's full system but eventually rejected his doctrine of God in favor of pantheism. Of the leading Chicago faculty, only Daniel Day Williams became and remained a full-fledged Whiteheadian.

Despite the wide range of agreement between those who followed Whitehead and those who did not, the gap between those who have continued the dominant Chicago tradition and those who have followed Whitehead has grown wider. Today the former group rarely identifies themselves as process theologians, leaving that title to the Whiteheadians. They are critical of Whiteheadian process theology for a variety of reasons. I will identify just two. First, it is too speculative and metaphysical. Second, it retains or recovers too close a relation with traditional Christian thinking and the churches. I will treat these concerns in succession.

That Whitehead's thought is speculative and metaphysical is not in question. Those who follow Whitehead recognize this and are grateful to him for having renewed this kind of philosophical thinking. For two hundred years most Western thinkers have eschewed this kind of philosophy. The neonaturalism of the Chicago school joined in this rejection. Wieman in his later years was especially explicit. To him it was crucial that theology be a description of (radical) empirically accessible reality. Any speculative element inherently made the assertions doubtful and shifted attention away from responding rightly toward debating doubtful ideas. This, he believed, was religiously disastrous.

I arrived at Chicago soon after Wieman left, but I was fascinated by his thought and wrote my master's thesis on it. My conclusion then, and now, was that he did not accomplish all that he hoped but that his thought is a permanent contribution of great value. I regret that it is not more widely studied today.

Wieman's greatest contribution, in my opinion, was his empirical demonstration that the process of creative transformation can be empirically described. Moreover, this description shows that, although creative transformation can be facilitated and served, it cannot be managed or controlled by human beings. On the other hand, I concluded that Wieman's thinking was not quite as free of dependence on speculative thought as he had hoped. It is possible to describe reality in ways that do not allow a place for what he had done. To follow Wieman requires rejection of these alternative views of reality. I agree with Wieman in this rejection, but among equally intelligent and careful thinkers there will be disagreements. One cannot escape this diversity of opinion by the appeal to the strictly experiential. I also concluded that, as a doctrine of God, his position did not quite work. Since in later writings he became less interested in whether the word "God" was used, this may not seem important. However, to me the question of whether life can be lived in relation to a reality that can be trusted is important. Wieman's claim to demonstrate this possibility appealed greatly to me. But if one is not allowed to speculate about what is going on in creative transformation, ontologically speaking, then the occasions in which it occurs have abstract similarities but no deeper unity. It is unclear just what one is called to trust.

The fact that elements of speculation seem inescapable, on the one hand, and that Wieman's limitation of speculation has negative consequences, on the other, confirmed me in my conviction that the intense and widespread rejection of speculation was misdirected. The quest for certainty is futile, and yet the fruitful life requires convictions. Accordingly, the goal should be to work toward the most probable conclusions, extensively guided, in my pragmatically oriented mind, by their implications for action. This judgment has led me to follow Whitehead.

It is noteworthy that following speculative thought further by continuing to ask questions leads, at least in Whitehead, to theories that connect more closely to historical patterns of Christian thinking and practice. That God needed to explain how and why the world has the character it has is quite different from what the official theology, profoundly influenced by the Greeks, has asserted. However, the God to which Whitehead's speculations led has remarkable congeniality with some strands of biblical thinking. This heightens the suspicion of many heirs of the Chicago school, but it strengthens conviction on the part of many of us who understand ourselves to stand in the Christian tradition.

I am not saying that all heirs of the Chicago school reject religious institutions and that all those who follow Whitehead are committed to them. But my impression is that the correlation is fairly high. Most Whiteheadian process theologians are church theologians. Most of the other heirs of the Chicago school are not. Hence their suspicions are justified. Perhaps some of us simply use Whitehead metaphorically as a fig leaf to continue with our unjustified childhood beliefs and wish fulfillments. Perhaps truly honest thinkers should distance themselves from all forms of church teaching.

For my part, I do not believe that seeking to be a follower of Jesus reduces the clarity or honesty of one's thinking. Also, I believe that more can be done to respond to the falsehoods and errors so often taught in the church when one is an active participant in its life. This in no way means that those who think about religious matters outside of religious communities fail to make important contributions to our society and to its institutions, including the religious ones.

Readers may be struck by the complete omission of Charles Hartshorne from this account. He, too, was a neonaturalist. But he was so different from the Chicago school that none of my discussion of the relation of Whitehead to that school applies to him.

What is the difference between Whitehead and Hartshorne?

The Chicago school has endured from the late nineteenth century until the early twenty-first century. Few theological "schools" have lasted that long. It could not have survived so long if it had been monolithic. In fact it has taken many forms and has been pursued in many ways. The school existed and flourished long before its members knew anything about Alfred North Whitehead. Its first phase is referred to as the sociohistorical school, whose most prominent leaders were Shirley Jackson Case and Shailer Mathews. They understood Christianity as a social movement that was to be viewed in a fully historical way.

This interest gradually gave way at Chicago to radical empiricism—"radical" in the sense that experience is not reduced to disconnected sense-data, but includes relationality and meaning. For the Chicago school, the focus was on the understanding of religious experience and locating God within experience. Henry Nelson Wieman was the leading exponent of this style.

Whitehead was of interest to both the sociohistorians and the empiricists. The former believed that science and democracy were the defining features of the culture in which the Christian movement should articulate its convictions. They considered it of first importance to understand the implications of the new science for faith. Whitehead's reflections attracted their attention. Wieman also followed the early thought of Whitehead with appreciation, and he taught Whitehead's philosophy at Chicago. However, as interest in Whitehead increased, Wieman became troubled by Whitehead's speculative approach. He determined to limit theological affirmations to indubitable elements of human experience. He defined God as the event of creative interaction or transformation, and called for trust in God, thus understood.

Nevertheless, Whitehead became increasingly important in the Chicago faculty. The third phase of the Chicago school was the Whiteheadian one. Some of the faculty became close followers of Whitehead. Others emphasized that Whitehead should be seen as one contributor among others to the ongoing task of constructing theology. Bernard Meland taught generations of students to think in cultural-historical forms, drawing on Whitehead but also on many other sources. Thus, even when Whitehead was the central figure, the neonaturalist school remained diverse.

None of these phases of the Chicago school focused on nature in distinction from human beings and human history. All of them rejected any metaphysical separation of human beings from the natural world. In this broad sense, they were all naturalist. However, none of them accepted the reductionism that typically accompanies the mechanistic metaphysics to which modern science bound itself. The Chicago faculty was very interested in scientific developments early in the twentieth century that pointed to a different understanding of nature, one that really could be inclusive of, or at least continuous with, human history. In the years after World War II, this new naturalism gave its name to the school. Whitehead provided its richest articulation.

Charles Hartshorne followed Whitehead extensively and emphasized the very side of Whitehead that Wieman turned against. Much of the influence of Whitehead in the Chicago school was due to Hartshorne. Students received a quite different understanding of Whitehead through the more empirically oriented faculty such as Bernard Loomer, Bernard Meland, and Daniel Day Williams. Thus considerable differences took root even among those who followed Whitehead to varying degrees. Such differences and variety continue to the present.

Many students received their fullest exposure to Whitehead through Hartshorne, but the works of the two philosophers exhibited marked differences. Some of the difference was due to their approach to philosophy. Whitehead came to philosophy largely to understand the abstractions that are the subject matter of mathematics and to resolve problems emerging from new developments in physics. He finally concluded that he needed to consider the knower as well as the objects of knowledge. This quest led him to develop a cosmology, by which he meant a synthetic vision of all of nature, including human beings. In doing so, he sought to distinguish between what must be true in all circumstances and what is particular to the universe in which we find ourselves. The necessarily true he called metaphysical.

Hartshorne, on the other hand, focused his primary attention on metaphysics from early in his life. He was drawn in this direction partly by purely intellectual interests, but also by religious concerns. He asked the traditional metaphysical questions and studied the history of their answers. He was sure that instead of declaring this discussion meaningless, as so many philosophers had decided to do, it was possible to advance the metaphysical project. For example, too often it was assumed that only two answers were possible to a metaphysical question. He showed that more were possible and that the best answer was often not among those from which metaphysicians had chosen in the past. This was a style of thinking quite different from anything that had been present in the Chicago school before Hartshorne came. It was also quite different from that of Whitehead.

What is surprising is that Hartshorne's metaphysics so extensively overlapped with Whitehead's and that it supported neonaturalism. Neonaturalism held, against idealism and dualism, that the human mind is continuous with the natural world. Hartshorne's metaphysics agreed.

Neonaturalism held, against materialism or any kind of pure physicalism, that nature was far richer and more complex than these reductionist views allowed. Hartshorne's metaphysics concurred. He taught what he called psychicalism, that reality at all levels was psychical in the sense of being composed of experiences. He implied what Thomas Berry has made explicit, that the universe is a communion of subjects rather than simply a multiplicity of objects.

Neonaturalism, at least implicitly, and often explicitly, criticizes the dominant scientific community for failing to break away from the older, materialistic form of naturalism. Hartshorne made significant contributions in showing how the focus on subjects can contribute to the enrichment and advance of science. His first book was *The Philosophy and Psychology of Sensation,* a contribution to physiology and psychology that has still not been assimilated into those disciplines. Late in his career he wrote *Born to Sing,* a book about birdsong that many ornithologists appreciate but few, as yet, follow. Both books were scientific expressions of a new naturalism. They are among the best examples we have of good science based on a much richer conception of nature.

Most streams of neonaturalism avoided or minimized explicitly metaphysical questions. Whitehead and Hartshorne did not. Yet their approach to metaphysics was quite different. Whitehead began with reflection on nature as science is now struggling to understand it and then moved on to broader and broader generalizations. The broadest of these were metaphysical. In this way he was closer to the empiricist traditions that dominated neonaturalism.

Hartshorne, in contrast, raised metaphysical questions directly and explicitly. This was so alien to the general style of neonaturalists that the term is often not applied to him at all. He used various labels for his position, but perhaps the most useful is "neoclassical" metaphysics. His critique of classical metaphysics was intense, but he asked the same questions and argued in familiar ways. His positions have become part of the debate in that small company of philosophers who give major attention to metaphysics. In particular, his work was in dialogue with traditional philosophical theology. In many of these discussions, the novelty of his understanding of nature is not so apparent.

In one respect, Hartshorne's thought was closer to that of the mainstream of neonaturalists than was Whitehead's. For Whitehead, abstractions, which are also pure potentials, played a large role in the description of the world. This reflects his mathematical orientation. He called these "eternal objects." Hartshorne, like the empiricist neonaturalists, belittled the eternal objects. He, too, wanted to stay closer to the concrete actualities.

Hartshorne shared with Wieman a desire to establish truths about which there could be no significant doubt, whereas Whitehead emphasized the hypothetical or speculative character of his thought. This represents less similarity than it might seem. Hartshorne found such certainties as Wieman established empirically to be of minor value or interest, and Wieman rejected the approach to truth through rational argument.

To summarize, the Chicago school, through all its periods and in all the forms it took in each period, can be called neonaturalist, but the positions adopted by its members varied greatly. Today these differences persist. Hartshorne played the double role of encouraging exacting study of Whitehead and of providing a distinctive version of neonaturalism. As we look to the future, the capacity of the Chicago school to survive in its diaspora rests in the diversity of traditions within it. This diversity is found even within the White-headian branch of the movement.

Has process theology "backed the wrong horse"?

William Placher, one of the brightest lights on the theological scene today, wrote a review of Gary Dorrien's third volume of *The Making of American Liberal Theology*. This volume covers the period 1950–2005 and is entitled *Crisis, Irony, and Postmodernity*.

Dorrien's treatment of process theology in its various forms is extensive and generous. The second chapter describes the Chicago school at the time I was a student there, picking up on extensive treatment of the earlier Chicago school in the preceding volume. The influence of the Chicago school is apparent in parts of every subsequent chapter.

Whitehead is, of course, only one of the sources of the Chicago school of this later period. Nevertheless, the volume makes clear the important role his thought has played. One chapter is devoted entirely to Whitehead and his influence. It begins with Norman Pittenger and devotes the rest of its space to the Claremont faculty and "process theology." Dorrien sees process theology as the form of liberalism most viable for continuation into the twenty-first century.

In response to this positive picture of process theology, Placher suggests in his review that Dorrien has "backed the wrong horse." This is not to say that Placher finds great promise in another form of liberalism. He is himself "postliberal." He finds the dependence of process theology on Whitehead's philosophy to be a particular liability. He pictures process theologians as having guessed that Whitehead's work would become central to American philosophy, so that connecting theology to it would give us status in the university. Insofar as any process theologian thought in those terms, she or he certainly mistook the situation. Whitehead's philosophy never became mainstream in graduate philosophy departments in the United States. Today it has virtually disappeared from the curriculum of the major philosophy departments. Understandably, observers will judge that we bet on the wrong horse—and hence have lost out.

Placher is certainly right in some respects. If American philosophers had increasingly accepted Whitehead, rather than marginalizing him, there would be far more process theologians today. Many theologians see it as important to be in conversation with the dominant schools of philosophy. When I was a young theologian, that concern led to great interest in existentialism and phenomenology. During the seventies and eighties it led to serious attention to Marxist social analysis. In the past two decades, it has focused many theologians on poststructuralism, which is also known as deconstructionism or postmodernism. These were the philosophical "horses" that "won" the races. Meanwhile, Thomist philosophies of various sorts have flourished among Catholics and among some conservative Protestants.

The question arises, then, why do some of us continue to rely on Whitehead's philosophy when the vast majority of philosophers ignore or reject his thought? Should we not bow to the authority of philosophers in judging what philosophy to follow? To say No seems arrogant, and perhaps it is.

Nevertheless, we were drawn to Whitehead by the depth of wisdom we found in his thought, not by its popularity among philosophers. We are more convinced now than then of that wisdom. Although his thought does not connect us to what goes on in departments of philosophy, it relates us to the cutting edge of the sciences in a way that other philosophies do not. That is one reason that, to us, it seems superior to the more widely accepted philosophies. We want a way of thinking that relates what we affirm as Christians to what the sciences are showing us to be true about the world, and we look more to science than to the major twentieth-century forms of philosophy for knowledge of this sort. Whereas in the twentieth century, philosophy more and more defined itself as one academic discipline among others, we hope that the twenty-first century will see a renewal of interest in comprehensive thinking about reality as a whole.

Our interest is not only in the natural sciences. It is in the social and psychological sciences as well. Human knowledge of human beings, their behavior, and their communities has exploded. It is at least as important that we integrate new knowledge in these fields with our theology as that we integrate knowledge of the physical world.

Some of those who reject our interest in Whitehead agree that we should pay attention to what some scientists have to say. But they see no need for a philosophical conceptuality in that process. If one needs to know more about social psychology, they argue, one should inquire of the social psychologists. To these theologians, it seems that bringing a philosophy into the picture complicates matters uselessly.

This makes clear a distinctive feature of process theologians. We believe that Whitehead has freed us from the bondage to a metaphysics that long distorted the appropriation of the biblical vision of God and the world. We believe that the sciences also are in bondage to an outdated metaphysics. For this reason we want to engage in revisionism in the natural and social sciences as well as in theology. We believe that revision is needed for the healthy development of the sciences. We are quite sure it is needed to develop further a unified vision of reality as a whole. This is a project we learned from Whitehead, and among philosophers he has virtually no rivals. Partial exceptions may be Teilhard de Chardin, Ken Wilbur, and some feminists, but in general their proposals for scientific revision are largely congruent with one another and with those of Whitehead. We continue to believe that Whitehead's thinking is the most fully developed.

It is our judgment, therefore, that the lack of acceptance of Whitehead among philosophers is not due to their success in pointing out philosophical weaknesses in his thought but to their defining the task of philosophy in ways that largely exclude his work from consideration. Related to this is that God plays an important role in Whitehead's philosophy, whereas the consensus among professional philosophers today is that one should not speak of God at all, and that if one does, one must at least deny to God any causal role. We continue to bet on Whitehead because we think he was right.

Claiming that Whitehead was "right" means that we think that most of what he said is accurate and true. For us, as for Whitehead, one important indicator of truth is usefulness. We find Whitehead's ideas immensely useful in formulating our Christian convictions and in understanding our Christian experience.

However, it would be a serious misunderstanding of the situation to think of Whitehead's usefulness only or even primarily in relation to reformulating traditional Christian teaching. One way of illustrating this point is to note that the one country in which Whitehead is definitely not marginalized today is China. Chinese Marxists are far more open to his theism than are most Western philosophers. However, his theism is not why they appreciate Whitehead and are trying to learn from him. They see his thought as giving a possible direction for China in its struggle to industrialize and democratize without losing its soul or destroying its environment. They are interested in the implications of Whitehead's thought for education, for psychological understanding, for legal theory, for agriculture, and for urbanization. All of this involves overcoming the dualism of nature and humanity and of object and subject that Western modernism has forced upon them. The Chinese hope to find a way toward the elusive goal of a sustainable society in which there is enough for all. Many of them see great promise in Whitehead's wisdom.

Of course, this Chinese interest in Whitehead may soon peak and wither. When the full radicality of the practical implications of Whitehead's thought for public policy is recognized, the Chinese government may silence it. On the other hand, Whitehead's ideas may have a great future in the world's largest nation. Through China, policies influenced by Whitehead's perspective may well spread to other countries.

Elsewhere, in both East and West, interest in Whitehead is increasing among people in many fields. Most promising for wider influence today may be quantum physics. A Whiteheadian type of quantum theory may pave the way to unification with a revised relativity theory. Meanwhile, Whitehead offers a third way in evolutionary thinking between the dominant neo-Darwinism and the supernaturalist alternatives. Whitehead also offers alternatives to the neoliberal economic thinking that has contributed so extensively to the fragility and ecological destructiveness of the global economy.

Whether the ruts we are now in, leading to chaos and destruction, are so deep that the proposal of alternatives is fruitless, we do not know. I would rather bet on the horse that offers a better way than on those horses that lead their vast following to destruction. As Christians, we are called to save the world. This today is an immensely practical matter. Until I find a way of thinking that promises more help in this task, I will continue to connect my theology to his thought. I believe there can be a great future for process theology.

PART TWO

Science

4

Evolution and Ecology

How does process theology respond to the challenge of modern science?

Process theology is critical of modern science, which distinguishes it from many other forms of (liberal) contemporary theology. Most accept the authority of the standard formulations of the natural sciences in their own domains. Process theology, as part of the broader movement of process thought, does not.

Process thinkers believe that modern science is wrong in many ways. It forces the evidence into a straightjacket that it derived from an external source. The straightjacket worked so well for so many purposes that the development of science greatly reinforced the hold it gained on the Western imagination. Indeed, we have come to call this straightjacket "the modern worldview." Process thought is a protest against that worldview and the proposal of another.

The dominant worldview during the Middle Ages was Aristotelian. Aristotle was the greatest scientist of his time, and his philosophy was open to further scientific progress. During the seventeenth and eighteenth centuries, the most influential scientists chose to follow Descartes instead. Descartes provided a different model of reality.

Aristotle emphasized the teleological or purposive element in the world and, therefore, explained things according to their functions or purposes. In reaction to this, the modern model rejected teleology in the natural world altogether. It emphasized efficient causes to such an extent that the word "cause" has come to mean what Aristotle thought of as just one type of "cause" among others. The efficient cause is the feature of the antecedent situation that necessitates what occurs in the present event.

If efficient causes explain events exhaustively, then we have no escape from complete determinism. Seeking exhaustive explanation, modern science is inherently deterministic. Given the limitation to efficient causes, the only alternative to complete determination by the past is random chance or blank ignorance.

From Whitehead's point of view, much has been accomplished by focusing on efficient causes and the mechanistically determined features of the world. But the reaction against Aristotelianism was too extreme and too dogmatic. A complete account of why any event occurs as it does requires both an account of the prior circumstances that impinged on it and a statement of how it responds to those efficient causes. The response is purposeful and plays its own role in deciding just what the new event will be. The refusal to allow any place to this element of purposeful self-determination has distorted and limited modern science.

The distortion is most obvious when scientific accounts of human action are offered. We know that we are not machines. Even providing scientific accounts of our actions is purposeful behavior. Scientists purposefully exclude purpose from their accounts of behavior that we know is purposeful.

From the perspective of process thought, animals also are purposive beings. The exclusion of purpose from scientific accounts of their behavior is also distorting. An account of the evolutionary process that does not include the role of animal purpose is incomplete and inaccurate. Unfortunately, the dominant scientific account has this character.

The basic model of the nonhuman world operative in the natural sciences is not only deterministic but also materialistic. Most moderns assume that the objects of touch and sight provide us with the basic paradigm of what is. These objects seem to exist self-identically through time. They are passive. They are related to one another only spatially and temporally.

This materialistic model has broken down in relation to the subatomic world. There it leads to conceptual chaos. Process thought proposes that matter be replaced by event as the fundamental character of reality. This would allow for reframing quantum theory in a much more intelligible way. Since the same ideas could then function in theories about the microcosmic and the macrocosmic worlds, more coherence can be introduced into science as a whole. To carry through this proposal requires extensive rethinking of science as a whole.

Particularly relevant to this question is evolutionary theory and its implication for the understanding of human beings and for belief in God. Whereas Descartes and many other early scientists assumed that the human mind was of a fundamentally different order from the objects they studied, evolutionary theory seemed to bring human beings fully into the scope of natural science. Given the dominant modern scientific model, including human beings implied that they, too, are to be understood in a deterministic and materialistic way. The implications for religion, ethics, law, politics, and daily life are staggering.

By replacing deterministic materialism with a model of events, largely determined by their antecedents but partly self-determining, process thinkers can offer an understanding of evolution that accounts better for the data. This model also yields an understanding of animals and human beings that accords much more closely with actual experience. Its implications for religion, ethics, law, politics, and daily life are far more reasonable.

Sadly, one reason for some scientists' rejection of process thought is that it opens the door to a theistic interpretation of the world. The exclusion of purpose from science was partly for the sake of removing God from relevance to nature. If, after all, purpose plays a role in nature, then God may be understood as the source of that purposive element in events. Indeed, that is the view of process theologians. To bring our religious insights and the empirical evidence together, we need to recognize that purpose plays a role in our lives and that this does not separate us from the rest of nature.

Does science support belief in God?

For most people who have studied science in high school and college, this question seems silly. Obviously, science as they studied it does not support belief in God. It would be a total violation of the rules of contemporary science, even of the way it is now defined, to introduce God into any explanation of what happens in the world.

If we are asking a slightly different question, the question of whether the findings of science, that is, our contemporary scientific knowledge, lend support to belief in God, the question is not silly. This tension between what has come to be understood as "science" today and the information that is gained by use of the scientific methods is worth exploring.

Like so many questions about the way we have been taught to think today, this one requires a little reflection about history. Modern science would not have come into being apart from belief in God. This belief gave thinkers confidence that behind or beneath the ever-changing flux of things were mathematically formulatable principles that explained what happened. To learn these principles would be to know something more about the mind of God. The early scientists repeatedly testified to their faith.

As these scientists succeeded in gaining knowledge of this kind, Christian thinkers began talking about the two forms in which God was revealed—the Bible, and nature. Both testified to the greatness and wisdom of the one creator.

At that time also the question of whether science supported belief in God would have seemed silly—but for the opposite reason. Almost by definition, science was the study of how God worked in nature. Scientists discovered more and more wonderful laws obeyed by nature, testifying more and more to the power and genius of the great lawgiver.

How did the change occur? In part, the advance of science was responsible. In the earlier stage of modern science, scientists discovered many different laws in every field they studied. Nothing about the physical things that obeyed these laws seemed able to explain why they did so. The physical world was understood to be composed of matter, and matter lacked any property of its own other than extension. As time went by, scientists discovered that many of these diverse laws were expressions of a much smaller number of very basic principles and that these principles could be understood as characteristics of nature itself.

A culminating instance of this was Einstein's theory of general relativity, or gravity. Newton's discovery of the law of gravity had been a major contribution to the early modern science that saw laws as imposed by God on a matter that had no principle of motion within itself. Einstein explained gravity as the very nature of space-time itself. Newton needed a lawgiver; Einstein did not.

A second change brought about by the advance of scientific knowledge was in the understanding of creation. When our ancestors asked how this marvelous world could have come into being, the natural answer was that a very powerful and very intelligent being created it. If we come across a watch in the desert, we are sure that some human being has been there. A watch cannot come into being by itself. The natural world is far more wonderful than a watch, and it certainly requires a creator.

However, if this very complex world evolved gradually over aeons of time from a much simpler one, the need for a creator diminishes greatly. The question is now whether a creator is needed to explain any of the steps in the long process of evolution—that is, are there gaps that can be explained only by external intervention? Scientists in general found the idea of such intervention fundamentally unacceptable. To exclude that possibility, they defined nature as a self-enclosed system. Although they acknowledged that explaining the emergence of life, and later of consciousness, was very difficult, they excluded in principle the idea that God was needed for this explanation. Scientists as a group had faith that science could eventually explain everything.

The new overarching evolutionary view accepted by science introduced a new issue. If human beings are a part of the nature studied by science, then does not nature include thought and purpose? A few scientists have answered this affirmatively, but the great majority has responded negatively and ruled the affirmative answer to be outside of science. They have retained the understanding of the world studied by science as lacking in any subjectivity. They have retained also the idea that the world is completely self-contained, that is, that everything that happens in this world can be explained by causes internal to it. Thus it is not only God who is excluded as explanatory of anything in the world; human purpose and intelligence is also excluded. The brain can play a causal role, but subjective experience cannot.

From the perspective of process thought, science has gone wrong here and has generated intolerable paradoxes. The decision to exclude the world of thought and feeling from playing a causal role is itself an act of conscious minds rather than of neuronal events as such. This decision has had enormous causal effects on the thinking and behavior of scientists. Yet all of this—thought, feeling, response, and purpose—must be denied by the scientists themselves, a denial that again is understood as physical events in the brain and hands and vocal cords not mediated by human thought or feeling. Indeed, in the name of science we are asked to affirm absurdities, even though science proposes the question not to us as conscious beings but to the neuronal activity in our brains.

If scientists as a group redefined science to be the study of both the objective and subjective worlds and their interactions, would that change the matter of support for belief in God? From the process perspective, it would. God acts in the becoming of every subject, that is, of every occasion of experience. Process theologians believe that the analysis of human experience reveals elements of novelty and purpose that can best be understood as the lure of God.

The objective world is made up of past occasions of experience. By influencing the way these occasions constituted themselves in the moment of their subjective existence, God has also influenced the objective events now studied by science. If scientists were open to this way of thinking of God's work in the world, would they find any evidence to support its hypothesis? I think they would. The evidence would be of three kinds.

First, although the many laws that once seemed to testify to the divine lawgiver have been shown to be what Whitehead called "habits of nature" rather than imposed on nature from without, at another level imposed universal regularities have been discovered. These are called "constants." Explaining these constants has led those scientists and philosophers committed to a self-enclosed nature into extraordinary violations of what were once supposed to be the limits of science. They now hypothesize the existence of innumerable universes to which we have no access whatsoever. These scientists and philosophers can then assert that the remarkable character of these constants can be viewed as a matter of chance. If these scientists and philosophers held no prejudice against introducing God into scientific explanation, they would find every reason to do so.

Second, scientists and philosophers can offer no explanation of how such constants affect what happens in the world. Where do such constants exist? What kind of status do they have to be able to play such an enormous causal role? Questions of this kind are rarely even asked. Whitehead did ask them, and his answer supported theism.

Third, the evidence appears to support an overall move in our universe in the direction of the realization of greater value. The constants are remarkable in that they are essential to the emergence of life, but they do not cause that emergence. They do not cause the proliferation of life forms or the emergence of central nervous systems. They do not cause the emergence of consciousness. The universe acts as if it favors subjective achievements of value where this is possible. The evidence supports theism.

Two major qualifications are needed. The first is very simple. I am claiming "support." Support is not proof. Process theology offers an understanding of God that fits coherently with what is known existentially, historically, and scientifically. I think that accepting this understanding of God illuminates much that is otherwise mysterious. It is also not unlike most scientific ideas. They, too, are not "proven," and sometimes new evidence or a new theory requires their modification. It is not given to human beings to have certainty. We cannot prove our own existence. We certainly cannot prove that of God.

Second, scientists have had good reasons to oppose opening the door to theism. In much of the Western tradition, God has been understood as omnipotent. The scientific evidence points to many causal forces in the world that are not in fact all controlled from one center. If God has causal efficacy in the world, scientists see God as one cause among others.

Furthermore, traditional Christian thought claims that God can overrule natural law and intervene at any time and in any way. Scientists see no evidence throughout history of any such intervention. Their whole sensibility would be violated if some example of such intervention were demonstrated. Process theism shares their sensibility. God is an essential factor in the way nature functions, not an external intervener in this process.

In short, the God whose reality can claim scientific support is not the God whose operation in the world science has defined itself to exclude. That exclusion was fully justified. Like so many justified acts, the exclusion was badly defined and understood. It is one of innumerable examples of throwing out the baby with the bathwater. The world that science studies does give evidence that a universal spiritual power exists and is intelligent and purposeful, working always and everywhere to realize what value there can be. Acceptance of that belief is no threat to the freedom of scientists or the advance of scientific research. Indeed, it could free science from the absurdities to which it has committed itself.

How do you deal with what is often called "ensoulment" in stem cell research–that is, at what point is an embryo a person?

The implications of process thought for the view of the embryo fall between the extremes represented by those who consider the embryo, and even the fertilized cell, to be a person and those who consider it simply a part of the woman's body over which she should have complete control. For process thought, the living cell is already something of value in itself, for itself, and for God and should therefore be respected by human beings as well. Organisms composed of many living cells have much greater value.

These multicellular organisms are of two types. One type establishes order among the cells through their internalized patterns of action and their relations with one another. This type is usually fixed in location. Plants are rooted in the ground and have no need of centralized control over movement.

The other type includes order of this kind but also has a centralized source of order. A unifying experience emerges out of the experiences of the cells in some part of the organism. This seems to require, at least for any stable occurrence, a central nervous system and a brain. Animals search for food and escape enemies. They need centralized direction to accomplish this.

In some instances the presence of any centralized control is disputable. Just how much brain is required for it to occur is also disputable. It is even possible that something of this sort can occur where there is no brain. However, most process thinkers judge that trees have no unifying experiences, whereas mice have the kinds of central nervous systems that do give rise to such experiences.

I have avoided the word "soul" thus far. In the public debate, this term is usually misleading. People assume that a particular organism either has or does not have a soul.

From a process point of view, some organisms clearly have no soul while in others souls clearly exist. A great many organisms, however, lie between these two extremes. This is true of embryos and fetuses throughout much of their development.

In the process perspective, the factual question that should be substituted for that about the soul when considering an embryo and its further development as a fetus is, strictly speaking, whether there are any occasions of experience that have the unifying function noted earlier. It is possible that in some organisms they occur sporadically, or only as needed. That would mean that much of the time the organism functions without any such unification. Even with normal human adults, it is not clear that any such occasions exist during dreamless sleep.

We should also note that occasions of this kind may have little connection. They may arise out of the nerve cells and influence them without deriving significantly from earlier unifying occasions or contributing to future ones. Even in a human baby, this seems to be largely the case at first.

The term "soul" or "person" is more appropriate when there is a succession of unifying occasions, each of which derives extensively from its predecessors and contributes extensively to its successors. Of course, each unifying occasion also derives from cellular occasions and contributes to them. The relative importance is always a matter of degree. Hence there is no one point at which the "soul" or "person" comes into being.

For process thinkers, then, there must be a first occurrence of an experience that unifies the cellular experiences in some region of the brain. It will be difficult ever to date such an occurrence. We can only say that it cannot occur until a rudimentary brain has been formed. But such an event is not the infusion of a soul. A fully developed soul, as described earlier, will not be present for some time after birth.

We need also to recognize that from a process perspective, souls are by no means unique to human beings. They are common throughout the animal kingdom. We should respect all ensouled animals, but that does not mean that they are never to be killed. Even vegetarians acknowledge that unless all carnivores are to starve, other ensouled animals must be killed. The unifying experiences of embryos and infants are less advanced than those of many animals that most people kill with little compunction.

In any case the question about ensoulment arises primarily with respect to human ensoulment. The soul does not become distinctively human until it engages in distinctively human symbolic activities. This hardly begins before language skills are developed.

This late emergence of the human soul, however, does not mean that the human fetus and embryo and newborn infant do not deserve our deep respect and protection. It means only that the respect and protection they require does not derive from their possessing human souls or being human persons. They deserve respect and protection, first, because they are of value in themselves, for themselves, and for God. This respect and protection are certainly not absolute. In and of themselves, their value is no greater than that of members of many other animal species.

An important difference distinguishes the human fetus and embryo and newborn infant from other otherwise similar organisms. In the case of a human embryo and fetus, these unifying experiences will develop, under favorable circumstances, into distinctively human souls. It is chiefly their *potential* value rather than their *realized* value that distinguishes humans from other animals from a very early point, even from the fertilization of the ovum. Indeed, one could even trace this back to the unfertilized ovum.

Obviously, this whole discussion presupposes the process perspective. For those who think in terms of substances, there has to be some enduring entity that is correctly identified as the human soul. The question of when ensoulment occurs then has to have a definite answer. Either the soul of this organism exists or it does not.

This is the way the topic was discussed in the church from ancient times. The church supposed that the soul, far from arising gradually out of the body and the cultural context, enters the soulless physical organism abruptly at some point. It was assumed that this was a creative act of God discontinuous with the natural order. Today the Catholic Church recognizes the arbitrariness of locating the origin of the soul at any specific point in the physical development of the embryo or fetus and has decided to assert that it is given together with the origin of human life, at the point of conception. This may avoid some forms of arbitrariness, but it introduces others. In terms of the historic and still common use of the term "soul," no evidence for its presence is available until much later.

From the process perspective, this doctrine may be the best one can do given the control of substance thinking. There is no escape from an arbitrary answer disconnected from empirical information. The consequence is a kind of absolutistic thinking that prevents reasonable judgments and blocks needed actions.

It is time to answer directly the question posed to me. I would say that embryos and fetuses are always potential human persons but never actual ones. The potential is very important and should never be thwarted casually, but it is not possible for all potentials to be actualized. Moral judgments consist in weighing values, one against another. That cannot be avoided.

With regard to stem cell research, we must weigh the gains that can be expected from such research against the destruction that it entails. As a practical matter, the destruction of realized value is quite slight prior to the development of the brain and the emergence of any unifying experiences. From that point on, it becomes greater. But this is more important for questions about abortion than about stem cell research. Here the question is almost entirely about the potential value of the embryo.

To produce embryos with the intention of killing them for research purposes is to me, personally, morally repugnant. That does not mean that there should be absolutist prohibitions. It does mean that I, personally, do not see sufficient justification for such a practice now. On the other hand, to use fetuses for research purposes that have been aborted for other reasons, ones that have no possibility of realizing their potential, seems to me, in and of itself, quite justified. The only negative that I see is that it may contribute to a further objectification and cheapening of life. In this respect it is not very different from much that we are already doing. The exact age of the fetus is not especially important in this case.

I was not asked about my overall view of this matter, but I will comment anyway. My basic judgment is that we use far too much of our resources on high-tech medical research and care that will benefit only a few, or make it possible for wealthy people to have children. To whatever extent the results of stem cell research will continue this pattern, I have no enthusiasm for it. If it could attain results that would benefit the masses of people who will never receive the benefits of high-tech medicine, I would favor it. But I doubt that this will occur.

Does process theology support those who promote "intelligent design" as explanatory of evolution?

A simple answer is possible. No. From the point of view of process theology, "intelligent design" is not a scientific theory and should not be presented as an alternative to the dominant theory of evolution. I say this first to avoid confusion about my position, because much of what I will say as I continue expresses a good deal of sympathy for this idea. My sympathy can be expressed by three basic points.

First, as a process theologian I do believe that divine intelligence affects the course of events generally, including biological evolution. This intelligence works purposefully and provides direction to the process. This is certainly close to the convictions of those who promote "intelligent design."

Second, process theologians do not believe that the standard teaching of biological evolution in our schools is adequate. The full reality of evolution is not explained by the mechanisms proposed in most biology textbooks. Revision is needed.

Third, this revision should avoid the reductionist character of current evolutionary theory in such a way as to overcome its systematic closure against the involvement of God in the process.

These points of agreement or overlap with advocates of intelligent design sharpen the question of why I oppose its teaching in the public schools. At the political level I do so because we have decided as a society not to promote any particular form of philosophical or theological thought in our schools. The phrase "intelligent design" implies almost necessarily a supernatural religious view, and most of those who promote it favor that kind of thinking. The teaching of science in public schools needs to stay closer to empirical evidence and testable theories. I would take this position even if I agreed fully with the theory of intelligent design.

Actually, the same need to avoid ideological teaching in the public schools underlies my objection to the currently dominant form of evolutionary theory. In this theory, the ideological element of modern science comes strongly and destructively to expression. Modern science early allied itself with a reductionist, materialist, mechanist model of the world. No scientific proof supports the truth or adequacy of this model. Process philosophy challenges this model. The currently dominant theory of evolution highlights the implications of this model because it so clearly posits that we human beings are a part of this world machine. This ideology should not be taught in public schools any more than intelligent design. Unfortunately, it is now implicitly taught with the authority of science.

Accordingly, as a process theologian, I am quite sympathetic with conservatives who want alternative theories taught. "Creationism," as such an alternative, failed to deal adequately with overwhelming bodies of empirical evidence. The theory of intelligent design is not so easily dismissed. In my opinion, its supporters do point to data that can more easily be understood on the assumption that there is a divine influence than on the assumption that the presently dominant model is adequate. Nevertheless, proponents of intelligent design move too quickly to a kind of explanation that falls outside the boundaries of science.

Further, as a process theologian, I do not agree with the theory of intelligent design. This theoretical level of the question may be of greater interest here than the political one. How does the view of process theologians that divine intelligence is at work in the world relate to the theory of intelligent design?

On the whole, the advocates of intelligent design accept the mechanistic view of the natural world. This leads to the position, long held by scientists and theologians alike, that God has imposed laws on nature. These laws express God's design for the world. The God who imposes these laws can also impose more particular patterns as needed.

Process theology need not wholly reject the notion of imposed law. Whitehead asserted that there has been and can be only one divine act that is unaffected by creaturely acts. This is the basic ordering of the eternal objects, the realm of possibility. God has imposed limitations on what will ever be actually possible in the universe. Today scientists talk about the physical "constants" and point out that if they were different, life could not have arisen in the universe. The ordering of possibility is the deepest ground of the order that gives rise to the notion of the laws of nature. It may channel developments in certain directions instead of others that in purely abstract consideration are equally possible. The ordering of possibility certainly expresses intelligence.

For Whitehead and those of us who follow him, the order of possibility works internally to every actuality. The world is not made up of bits of matter that are set in motion along predetermined routes from without. The world is made up of partly self-determining events, each of which decides among those options that are made possible by the divine ordering of possibility, given the actual world in that moment.

The word "design" is misleading in this context. It suggests an imposed outcome rather than one that is the joint result of the primordial divine decision and many creaturely ones. Within the limitations imposed by God's decision, there are numerous genuinely possible directions for the course of events to follow. Evolution need not have produced human beings. Nevertheless, the basic order of things is such that this specific outcome was possible and that there is a general tendency to produce organisms capable of greater intensity and complexity of experience.

I am not advocating that the process view of God's role in evolution be taught in public schools. What I do advocate is that the diverse elements contributory to evolution be recognized. Today the focus is almost entirely on random genetic changes, with the rare beneficial ones selected by environmental factors. But there are many indications that the activities of organisms also play a large role in evolution. This is true from the cell through to human beings. It is hard not to suppose that the preference of so many biologists for explanation in terms of random mutations, rather than the choices of individual organisms, is ideological rather than scientific in any idealized or normative sense.

From the point of view of intelligent design, a change in the way that evolution is interpreted scientifically might not make much difference. From the point of view of process theology, it would make a great difference. The current teaching of evolution implies ultimately that human beings are nothing but matter in motion. Human purpose and intelligence is basically an illusion, simply a by-product of mechanical forces with no causal influence in the world. If, in contrast, it were recognized that every action of every entity has some effect on the evolutionary process, however trivial, the implication would be entirely different. At the human level, the effect on the evolutionary process is far from trivial.

The vision would be that every event is extensively, even primarily, shaped by its past but, nevertheless, has some element of self-determination, however slight. This becomes more significant in more complex creatures. This self-determination is selection among those possibilities provided for it by God's ordering. Creaturely purpose and divine purpose appear together in this vision.

Where to draw the line in terms of what is taught in school is harder to decide from the process perspective. I believe, however, that the scientific evidence indicates that creaturely activity influences the evolutionary process and that this should be taught. I believe the evidence indicates that at advanced levels, this creaturely activity is intelligently purposeful. I believe that scientists can acknowledge that, even at lower levels, it is sometimes functional and underdetermined by the circumstances, which means it is purposelike.

I believe scientists can acknowledge that in the process of evolution, new properties emerge that change the nature of the whole process. This means that the reductive commitments of the traditional model should be given up. Newly emergent properties act back upon the entities from which they have emerged. Most importantly, psychic or mental events not only are influenced by physical ones but also influence them. In my opinion, if scientists examined the evidence without a strong ideological bias in favor of reduction, they could teach such causal relationships without abandoning the limits of science.

I realize, of course, that this would be an enormous change and one that would prove very difficult for many scientists to accept. Many would object as vehemently to such changes as to the teaching of intelligent design. However, I do not take the opposition of scientists as a reason for not pushing for such teaching in public schools. The issue in this case is that of empirical evidence. If the evidence does not support emergence and what can be called top-down causation, scientists should not teach these theories. But if the evidence does support them, and only deeply established ideology prevents their inclusion, we have the right to demand at least that alternative theories be taught.

I would like to imagine that some day it would be possible to talk about God in scientific discourse. That is not possible today. One may talk about the physical constants that make life possible, but one cannot describe these as a divine decision. I am hoping that we can move to a situation in which the actions of organisms, including intelligent and purposive actions, can be recognized as playing an important role in evolutionary development, but for the foreseeable future we cannot talk about any divine influence on those actions.

Part of the problem is that the word "God" is so bound up with supernaturalism that God's role in natural processes cannot be considered without violating science. When considering what can be taught in public schools, this limitation must be respected. Either under this term or under some other, perhaps "divine Spirit," we can in our own circles speak in ways that bring our knowledge of the natural world and our understanding of deity into mutually supportive and illuminating relationships. Perhaps someday that would allow us to educate our children in a more holistic or inclusive context.

What does process theology have to say about "inconvenient truths"?

The fate of the Earth is the overarching question, the context in which we should consider all other questions. Process thought supports, if it does not require, the view that all other issues are subordinate to this one.

The dominant worldview of the modern world has been dualistic. It has separated nature from the distinctively human. The organization of knowledge in the university expresses this view, carrying the boundaries further into extreme fragmentation. This dualism and fragmentation play a pervasive role in blocking thought and action appropriate to the planetary crisis.

Since the university has accepted Darwinian evolutionary thinking, this dualism makes little sense. For a Darwinian there can be no such separation of the human from the natural. Dualistic habits are deep, and the university and Western thought generally have ignored the contradiction between acceptance of Darwin and ignoring the fundamental implications of such acceptance. What we know from the natural sciences still has only the most indirect influence on the humanities and even on the social sciences.

There are exceptions. A good many philosophers now explain human phenomena by reducing them to expressions of physical phenomena. A good many scientists, especially evolutionary biologists, argue that in fact we humans are nothing but part of the material, mechanical nature of nineteenth-century physics. Although this materialistic reductionism overcomes dualism, it is hardly a helpful response. It abolishes all questions of value. Although in principle this kind of scientism might teach how threatened the world is by human actions, it provides us with no reason to care.

Process thought is one form of an alternative that hovers around the edges of the university and plays a somewhat larger role in Western culture generally. In this view, humanity is part of nature, a very distinctive part. Nature is not, however, composed of matter in motion. It is composed of organisms that have reality and value in themselves and for one another. What happens at one point has effects elsewhere. The inordinate increase of human population and the extraordinary power that humans have attained to manipulate other parts of nature and even themselves pose unprecedented threats to the whole of the biosphere.

As in the case of evolution, some of these facts are not denied by scholars in many fields, but they are ignored. Business as usual means acting as if they were not true. Remaining in well-established disciplinary ruts supports the business interests that also act as though these facts were not true. However, a worldview shaped by process thought makes the degradation of the biosphere much harder to ignore.

In the late 1960s, it seemed that a breakthrough to basic change might occur. Earth Day 1970 was a wake-up call of great promise. The national government was affected. Good legislation was passed. It seemed that even the university might change.

This brief time of promise passed quickly. Within a decade, popular pressure to respond to the crisis faded, and the country was firmly under the control of those who were determined to act as if the problem did not exist. They did not deny that *problems* existed, but they decided to deal with these problems piecemeal in ways that did not disturb our "way of life." The university returned fully to the ruts that had briefly been challenged. Environmental concerns became one specialty among others or were located at the margins of a variety of disciplines. The fate of the Earth was no longer studied.

The churches added the evil of environmental destruction to the long list of ethical concerns. This addition was important. But the overwhelmingly anthropocentric character of our liturgies and preaching was not changed except that, on one Sunday each year, many churches turn their attention to the Earth. This concern plays little role except when someone reminds others that it should not be forgotten.

My own awakening came in 1969. When I realized that the future of life on the planet was threatened, all other concerns seemed secondary. Under that impression, I said and did some things of which I am now not proud. I have not changed my mind, but I rather quickly came to see that efforts to respond to the crisis of the natural world that displayed, or seemed to display, insensitivity to issues of justice were wrong in themselves and would only make matters worse. The only hope was a more holistic approach to the world's problems. The term "eco-justice," widely used by Christians in those days, pointed in the right direction. This was also a better fit with process thought.

I soon decided that the little I could do fell into two related areas. First, I could work harder to promote the nondual vision of reality. Since I believe that Whitehead had the most fully developed and profound version of this vision, I identified myself and my work more fully as being the promotion of his thought and its implications.

Second, I became convinced that economic behavior was the place where overcoming dualism was most important. The dualistic behavior was supported by dualistic theory. I hoped that exposing the profound inadequacy of the assumptions on which the world's economy was based might help to slow the headlong rush of humanity to self-destruction. Unfortunately, because those inadequate ideas prove so profitable to the rich in the short run and are so deeply entrenched in the university, they play an even greater role in the world now than then.

I can report some progress. More and more people reject dualism and seek to view reality in nondual ways. The promotion of Whitehead's thought has contributed to this improvement. Also, more and more people recognize the damage done by the present form of economic organization and actions. Many of them recognize that standard economic theory has proven a bad guide. More and more people and groups, at the periphery of government, business, and the university now subscribe to an alternative way of organizing the economic world that could be just and sustainable. They affirm that another world is possible. Thus far, the alternative vision has had virtually no effect on the basic patterns of global activity and planning. It has, however, won enough popular support in some parts of the world to slow down the destructive juggernaut. It has blocked the advance of the FTAA (Free Trade Area of the Americas) and of the WTO (World Trade Organization). It has also led much of South America to refuse the continuation of U.S. domination and exploitation. These are real gains.

But as overall human activities have become more destructive of the planet and opposition has slowly mobilized, the crisis has grown and become more imminent. In 1970 I wondered whether it was already too late. Computer predictions of disaster tended to indicate 2020 as the time when collapse would begin. That gave us fifty years to change our ways. Four fifths of that time has passed, and we have not adopted better policies.

Perhaps we have decisively squandered our chance. James Lovelock thinks so. His recent book, *The Revenge of Gaia: Earth's Climate Crisis and the Fate of Humanity,* opens with the words "Now is much too late." He compares the view that we could now save the biosphere, including the human population, from collapse by stopping our destructive activities with the idea that a lung cancer victim can be cured by stopping smoking. Like the predictions of the book *Limits to Growth* decades ago, he foresees a drastic reduction of the human population.

Lovelock's analysis should not be dismissed lightly. He has often been right in the past. Even he does not advocate that we simply plan how to respond to the total disaster we face. He hopes we will "get real." For example, whereas I and many other environmentalists have opposed nuclear power because of its enormous long-term dangers, he advocates it because, in the short run, which should now concern us decisively, it has the best chance of reducing the use of fossil fuels and thereby slowing global warming. Perhaps he is right. To the current threat we cannot seek *good* solutions. There are none.

Perhaps Lovelock and others can awaken us to the extreme urgency of drastic action. Perhaps we will be prepared to compromise with respect to what that action should be. At this point our deepest convictions will come into play. If humanity faces catastrophes of dimensions never known before, what are the implications for us?

The first implication is that responding to this overarching danger takes priority over almost all other considerations. Liberals and Christians have too often opposed needed actions on moral grounds. For example, in China, drastic action to slow population growth was of critical importance, and the government responded intelligently. American liberals and many Christians expended more energy in pointing out the infringement of personal liberties and increased abortion of female fetuses than in supporting the basic policy. To this date, the Catholic Church and many Protestants do not support even moderate efforts to reduce population growth, believing that these conflict with moral principles or divine laws. Yet any objective analysis shows that the vast increase in the human population in the past century has contributed significantly to hastening the impending catastrophes in which billions of people are likely to die.

Second, in October 2003 the Office of Net Assessment of the Department of Defense published a study responding to this question of implications, *An Abrupt Climate Change Scenario and Its Implications for United States National Security*. The study foresees a time in the not-distant future when weather changes will cause billions of people to struggle over the remaining resources and to seek refuge in still habitable places. Accordingly, we should be militarily equipped to protect what we have and secure more, regardless of the number of people we have to kill in the process. The response of the Department of Defense to the prospects of global catastrophe is a military one. What about ours? Is there an alternative? If our remaining resources are sparse, can we advocate sharing them with those who have still less? Would anyone survive such sharing?

These are morally unanswerable questions. The alternative is to think in a quite different way. Since the problem is global and not national, the reflection should also be global and not national. What can be done globally to reduce the coming disasters and mitigate their consequences? How can we prevent the wasting of resources in military conflicts and mutual slaughter? How can we work for a decent world for the survivors?

We Americans, or at least our leaders, have been most resistant to genuine discussion and decision at the global level. Accordingly, those of us who believe that our behavior has been profoundly damaging to the prospects of a livable world have a special responsibility to all humanity to do what we can to change our government's priorities.

Does process theology offer a word of hope? Yes, a very conventional one: God. Process theology does not, however, hope for supernatural intervention. God acts only by calling creatures to act. Our hope is that key people at key times will respond to God's call so that God can work through them to save what can still be saved of the beauty and glory and habitability of this planet. Since leaders cannot effect redirection of policy and action without followers, we can all be responsive to God's call now, and again and again, to think and act in light of the reality of our planetary situation. That call is always particular to the particular situation of the one who is called. That God can break through our all-too-willful blindness and the hardness of our hearts is the hope that sustains us.

5

Economics

The Wall Street financial crisis seems to be a "teachable moment." Generally, eyes glaze over when one talks about economics, and especially about finance. This time, people evidence some desire to understand what is happening.

One can discuss this at different levels. In Congress and in the press, the discussion is about how to get the normal financial functioning of the United States back on track. Since the most dramatic expression of the financial system's derailment is on Wall Street, attention is focused on how to get Wall Street firms to begin operating normally again. Given that level of discussion, there is little doubt that a solution favorable to Wall Street will be found and implemented.

Around the edges, another discussion centers on whether the money might be spent in ways that would benefit more people. For example, we could focus on helping people who are unable to pay their mortgages. This plan would keep people in their homes and keep money flowing to the immediate lenders, even if not at the high interest rate they anticipated. It would hasten the recovery of the housing market but would not cost nearly as much money. Lending agencies and banks would not expect to recover the money in the future, except indirectly through the expansion of employment and a better property tax base.

It is not clear which of these approaches would actually free up credit more rapidly. It *is* clear that Wall Street, rather than at-risk homeowners, controls the media. Fear of financial collapse generated by those Wall Street controls–including most of the government–will decide the issue.

Christian theology in general favors a government not controlled by the financial sector but able to act for the benefit of the weaker members of society. Certainly, process theologians share this bias. So we are not happy about the fresh display of Wall Street's power, but we are not surprised. Wall Street owns the so-called Federal Reserve Bank. The secretary of the treasury is now, as almost always, a Wall Street banker. Wall Street is the largest funder of those running for office in both parties, having given this time a bit more to Obama than to McCain. We should not be surprised that our government would be prepared to go to great lengths to salvage Wall Street from the consequences of its excesses.

Most economists, but far from all, tell us we had no choice. Looking simply at the financial sector, they may be correct that saving Wall Street will reduce panic more than any other measure. A theologian is not in good position to judge.

Process theologians can, however, play another role. Whereas the vast majority of economists are socialized to consider how best to keep the current system functioning, theologians are free to ask about the system as a whole and its alternatives. They may even wonder about the possibility of something more like "biblical economics." Process theologians claim to be freed from the distorting glasses with which the Bible and subsequent history have been read in the mainstream of Western theology. From our perspective we can ask about the assumptions of the present system and evaluate these in light of the Bible. Consider the following assumptions that now shape our world.

1. The basic goal of the social and political order is to serve the economic order.
2. The goal of the economic order is to promote overall increase in production and consumption.
3. Such increase is best achieved by privatizing all activities that can be pursued for profit, as well as all the resources used by business.

4. The market should be as large as possible and as free from regulation as possible.
5. Credit based on interest payments to financial institutions should also be free from interference by the government.
6. These institutions rather than government should create money to expand the money supply and should reap the profits from this activity.
7. Justice, community, personal happiness, and the condition of the natural world are irrelevant.

A world organized in this way will have predictable consequences. For some time, it will succeed in its goal of increased production. In the process, existing communities will be broken up and new ones will be transient. The global ecology will deteriorate rapidly and dramatically.

The achievement of these goals will greatly increase the gap between the rich and the poor within nations and between nations. The lot of the poor will become more miserable as governments are discouraged from having concern for them. Those who gain great wealth also gain great power, and this power will be used to push forward the policies that have made them rich.

As wealth is concentrated and made mobile, the importance of the financial sector will increase. Actual production becomes secondary as a means of gaining wealth in comparison with financial manipulation. As financial institutions are freed from governmental regulations, they will center even more economic power in themselves. Governments will assist them in further concentration of wealth.

The contrast with biblical and traditional Christian thinking could hardly be more glaring.

1. Economic activity should serve human beings and their social and political institutions.
2. This means that the economy should be so organized as to strengthen human community and develop a sustainable relationship to the environment.
3. Which activities should be private and which public is to be decided pragmatically.
4. In general, the market should be as local as possible so that it can serve the local community. How much regulation by the community is needed is to be decided pragmatically.

5. Justice, community, personal happiness, and the condition of the natural world are the primary considerations.

I have omitted biblical statements about the financial sector. Whereas I believe that nations could order themselves according to the five biblical principles enunciated earlier, the teaching of the Bible about finance seems utopian. The Bible forbids interest on loans. Efforts to observe this prohibition have led more to ways to circumvent it than to a genuine alternative.

Nevertheless, the biblical vision is important to recall. Again and again, in biblical times and since, a relatively egalitarian distribution of resources, chiefly land, has been undercut as money lenders have taken advantage of critical needs of small landowners to lend money that they cannot repay. Widespread ownership has been superseded by concentrating wealth in land ownership. Classically, workers have often had to sell themselves as well to survive. Ethically concerned observers railed against this transformation of healthy community into a class society. Since the interest on loans is what usually makes it impossible to repay, they focused their opposition on that. Jesus taught us to pray for the divine commonwealth (the "Kingdom of God") in which all debts would be forgiven, as in the year of Jubilee.

The contrast between this opposition to finance, on the one side, and giving primacy to the financial sector, on the other, is marked indeed. To propose the abolition of interest seems quite useless. Still, we may let the Bible inspire us to envision a quite different overall economic system from the present one in which debt plays the primary role.

One destabilizing feature of the debt economy is that debts overall cannot be repaid at interest except as the money supply is increased enough to make it possible. This increase of money supply is currently left to banks. The banks collectively receive the interest on the money they create by their loans. Their ability to make loans far in excess of deposits is what enables them to create money and be paid interest on their creation. Over time this guarantees that wealth will be concentrated in their hands.

In principle, banks share the power with governments to create money. However, jealous of their prerogative, they often exclude the government from exercising its ability. The British colonies in North America spent and loaned money into existence and enjoyed considerable prosperity as a result. The Bank of England persuaded

Parliament to forbid this, plunging the colonies into depression. This had more to do with their revolutionary fervor than the tax on tea.

The Continental Congress financed its successful struggle for independence from Britain by creating money. A major strategy of the British, too late in its success to stave off defeat, was to flood the colonies with counterfeit money to such an extent that people lost confidence in "the continental." This loss of value gave credence to the view that national currency should be backed by gold, and the U.S. government was, accordingly, restricted in its creation of money. Lincoln understood that no such backing was really needed, and he successfully financed the Civil War by spending money into existence with no metal backing.

Nevertheless, the bankers succeeded in persuading the public that a government should not do this. They persuaded Congress to create the "Federal" Reserve Bank, largely owned by Wall Street, to issue currency, which gradually replaced treasury notes. Later, they happily abandoned the gold standard. We have returned to the sort of money used by the Continental Congress and Abraham Lincoln, but now we have to pay the banks for the privilege of spending it. An increasing portion of our national budget goes to servicing a debt that results from our government turning over to the banks all power to create money.

There is a radical alternative. We could require that lending institutions lend only the money that their depositors entrust with them. This would then leave all creation of money in the hands of the government. The government could then both spend and lend into existence the amount needed for the economy to function. The result could be an end to government borrowing and a great deal more freedom for the government to take care of infrastructure, education, health care, and social services. Banks would become service institutions to society rather than concentrations of wealth and power.

To take another step into a biblical economy, the government could institute a special program to lend moderate amounts to individuals who are in financial trouble. This program might include financial guidance and access to special funds as well as simply making money available. Its goal would be to prevent foreclosure or bankruptcy.

Obviously, radical changes of this sort in the financial sector are not now "on the table." But let us suppose that we bail out Wall Street and restore some regulations. Suppose, then, that as the situation improves, once again Wall Street persuades Congress to free it from onerous limitations. Then suppose we endure another boom-and-bust cycle. Perhaps Wall Street can again persuade the public to bail it out. We learned very little from the earlier savings-and-loan crisis. Perhaps we will forget about this one too. But perhaps not. Public resistance this time has been surprisingly intense. If the availability of a very different financial system is widely known, it might gain substantial support. Miracles are possible.

Can process theology shed light on the 2008–2009 financial meltdown?

No direct route leads from how we think about God, the world, and human well-being to the interpretation of a complex socio-economic phenomenon. On the other hand, how we understand and respond to such a phenomenon is deeply affected by our whole way of understanding and thinking.

This has been quite apparent. For the dominant sector of society, the meltdown of the "paper economy" and leading financial institutions called for emergency steps to restore them. The initial proposal worked out by Wall Street bankers in the government with those still on Wall Street was simply to give public money to Wall Street while guaranteeing that bankers would not be prosecuted for the questionable acts that brought about the crash. Congress modified this inner Wall Street proposal but did not challenge its assumption that the basic system is to be restored.

The alternative proposal was to go a different direction in using the money Congress was prepared to pay Wall Street. The alternative plan would spend the funds to support the "real" economy, that is, to help homeowners keep their homes and provide credit to businesses. The bill as finally passed allowed for some of this, although the decision as to how to spend the money was left in the hands of Wall Street bankers. Clearly the difference between top-down thinking and bottom-up thinking makes a practical difference! Clearly, also, those who follow Jesus, whether influenced by process thought or not, support the latter.

Why does top-down thinking dominate? One reason is obvious. The top is more powerful than the bottom. Rarely can anyone be elected to a national office without the support of the top. This is because the top not only supplies most of the money needed to run for office but also controls the media from which most of the electorate receives its (dis)information. The top controls the leadership of both the major parties.

The other reason is not as widely recognized: Ideology is very powerful. The dominant ideology supports the top. Actually, the situation is worse than that. Our system has only one well-articulated ideology. It is called "neoliberalism." It teaches that government exists primarily to serve the economy and the goal of the economy is growth as measured by gross domestic product. Growth is best achieved by privatizing almost everything, removing government regulations, ending government interference in the market (subsidies and bailouts), freeing capital to move globally, and keeping labor docile.

Basically, the leadership of both political parties subscribes to this ideology. The Democrats are more likely to moderate their application of this ideology with concerns for the effects on workers and the environment. But under Democratic leadership, NAFTA (the North American Free Trade Agreement) was passed, and banks were freed from the Glass-Steagall Act, whose provisions would have at least sharply limited the financial meltdown. The Republicans are more likely to support government involvement in the economy when that means massive giveaways to large corporations, but many Democrats support these, too.

Many people are critical of this ideology, and especially of the ways in which it is implemented. Globally, they have expressed this criticism by throwing off the shackles of the IMF (International Monetary Fund) and blocking expansion of the WTO (World Trade Organization). But they have not developed an alternative ideology. In the United States many people want to reregulate the banking industry, increase social spending, and give some priority to environmental concerns; but they have no alternative ideology.

In the 1980s, I worked with Herman Daly, a Whiteheadian economist, to show that the philosophical assumptions underlying the now dominant ideology are, at least from a process perspective, mistaken or inadequate. We proposed an alternative set of assumptions, such as that the economy should serve human community rather than destroy it, that justice should play a role in basic economic thinking, and that sustainability is of crucial importance and requires careful attention to the natural environment of human economic activity. Much more work is needed to develop our suggestions.

The reigning ideology treats economics as a science and simply expects the other dimensions of life to be subordinated to it. Our process alternative argues that economics is not a science and that economists should redirect their thinking to the support of a just and sustainable society. This means that economic theory, as such, cannot become the overarching ideology. The ideology needs to view social, cultural, religious, psychological, political, and economic matters in their interconnectedness and understand them all in historical terms. Further, this new ideology needs to locate human history in the context of the history of life on this planet. Nowhere in our universities is this kind of thinking encouraged. Hence we are at a considerable disadvantage in opposing the now-dominant ideology.

How does all of this relate to the financial crisis? First, it indicates that finance should serve the real economy, which should serve the well-being of the world. Viewed in this light, financial institutions have become an almost total failure so that we have no justification for trying to prop them up. We can deal with the real need of the world for finance with far simpler and more limited institutions. Individuals and businesses have a real need to be able to borrow for constructive purposes, such as buying homes and expanding businesses. But in recent years a great deal of borrowing has been for purposes of making money out of financial transactions as such, without regard to the effects on the real economy. We see no reason to make further sacrifices to enable people to live on the profit from this kind of speculation.

Viewing matters historically helps. As long as people borrow money and pay interest on it, it is necessary to increase the money supply. Through much of history this was done by rulers, that is, by governments, creating the needed money. They could do so simply by spending it, so that governments could and can finance much of their activity simply by creating the money to do this. The American Constitution envisions this financial system. Some of the colonies had employed it until the Bank of England persuaded Parliament to forbid the colonies from creating money.

In the United States, private banks have taken over the government's power to create money. They create money by lending it at interest. They lend out many times the amount of money deposited by savers. The more money loaned out at interest, the greater is the need for additional lending to supply the money to pay the interest. Thus most of the profit of the banks comes from their creation of money. This is fundamental to the financial system in this country. If the government recovered the money-creation function, it could reduce both the debt and taxes, while rebuilding the nation's infrastructure and providing better health care.

This would mean the end of the fractional reserve system, which is banking as we have known it. Banks would only be able to lend the money that their depositors entrust to them, making their profit by collecting more from borrowers than they paid depositors. The government could still insure deposits, so that banks could lend most of the money deposited in them without fear of a run. If the credit thereby provided proved insufficient, the government could supplement with its own banks. The Federal Reserve Bank, which despite its name actually belongs to Wall Street, could be either turned into a national bank or abolished.

Needless to say, opposition to any moves in this direction would be enormous. What in the nineteenth century was called the "money power" would not yield its privileged place in society easily. Only a much more extensive unraveling of the financial sector might open the way to dramatic change. Even then, the proposals I am making could occur only if a significant segment of the public was prepared support them.

The financial sector now dominates the economy and the politics of our nation. It speeds the concentration of wealth in fewer and fewer hands, while contributing nothing to the common good. The most powerful members of this sector are using the present crisis to further concentrate power. We will find that some leaders will press for further reduction of social services in light of the increased national debt and even for further removal of federal regulations of the financial sector.

Nevertheless, the collapse of the financial bubble provides an occasion in which more people may learn how the "money power" has monopolized the wealth that should belong to all of us. A collapse may be the occasion when a political move for the government to recover this power becomes a real possibility.

PART THREE

Faith

6

Christology

The affirmation of incarnation is central for Christians. Few people would dispute that statement. Many would dispute how to understand and express incarnation. Many Christians understand it to mean that a God, who is otherwise "other" and remote, once broke into history to reveal a nature that is otherwise hidden and to act for our salvation. Some of those who interpret incarnation in this way affirm it quite straightforwardly as a supernatural event. Others assume that it is a mythological teaching. Of these, some reject it accordingly; others find rich meaning in the myth. Still other Christians, and this includes those of us influenced by process thought, understand Christianity as an incarnational faith, meaning that it affirms that God is incarnate in the whole world. For us, "incarnation" does not point to a single supernatural act of God. It points to the basic nature of God's relation to the world, a relation that is made fully manifest in Jesus.

For the first group, the background idea, shared with those who wrote the classical creeds of the church, is that each entity is fundamentally self-enclosed. Philosophically, we can think of everything as a substance—in Greek, ousia. The problem is that substances can act on one another only from without. No two substances can occupy the same space at the same time. Accordingly, the divine substance

107

cannot occupy any of the space occupied by the human substance of Jesus. God and creatures, including the human Jesus, can only be external to one another.

Despite this fundamental conceptual problem, the early church was convinced that God was incarnate in Jesus. This suggests that the divine substance occupies the same space as the human substance of Jesus. To avoid saying what could make no sense in their categories of thought, some theologians proposed that some part of the human substance was replaced by the Divine. An early suggestion was that while the body of Jesus was human, his soul was divine. Fortunately, the church rejected this idea. Other efforts of this sort were made. The last such proposal that occurred during the formation of the creeds was that in Jesus the divine will replaced the human will. We may be thankful and proud that the church fathers were not willing, in this or any other way, to regard the human substance of Jesus as lacking anything. They insisted that Jesus was fully human as well as divine.

The effort to locate God in Jesus by denying some human property to Jesus continued despite the creedal affirmations. It expressed the impossibility of making sense of incarnation given the metaphysics of substance that everyone accepted, consciously or unconsciously. Sadly, a final proposal, never debated in an ecumenical conference, was widely accepted in both East and West. This proposal claimed that the "person" of Jesus, what Jesus meant when he said "I," was God. Jesus' humanity was lacking in this unifying personal center. It was "impersonal." The church has suffered greatly from this denial of Jesus' full humanity.

I rehearse this history to indicate the consequences of trying to understand incarnation in the categories that still, unconsciously, shape the thinking of most Western people. The positive way of putting the result is that the incarnation is a "mystery." In my view, however, the common doctrine of incarnation is a mystification and distortion made necessary by the philosophical assumptions of those who developed it. I certainly do not blame them for having had only those categories to work with. Given that fact, I marvel that they for so long steadfastly held to God's real presence in a real human being. I keenly regret the subsequent qualification of Jesus' humanity, which for many has led to the supposition that Christians see Jesus as God in impersonal human form rather than as a true and genuine human being in whom God was incarnate.

In the twentieth century, I am glad to say, talk of incarnational thinking expanded. Theologians viewed the world in new ways. God is not seen as remote but as present in us as well as to us through other creatures. This picks up on Paul's vision that we are in Christ and Christ is in us. The Spirit is also in us. Still, even in the twentieth century, most interpreters of Paul have preferred to emphasize "justification by faith" as central to his thought, since this did not involve ideas of real participation in Christ. Substance metaphysics still influences Christian teaching and blocks appropriation of biblical ways of thinking.

Whitehead's thought provides us with an alternative conceptuality that removes these obstacles. For Whitehead, a moment of human experience is to be understood as an example of what *is*. This is not a self-enclosed substance but an ingathering and creative synthesis of the world that is inherited. This world is constituted by its inclusion of others. To be is to take others into oneself.

One of the others incorporated in each moment of experience is God. Thus God is quite literally present in every experience. Such incorporation can be called immanence. It can also be called incarnation. Thus this philosophy provides us with an incarnational view of all things.

The fit with the Bible is far better. However, one can argue that those who hold an incarnational view of the world can no longer see anything distinctive in the incarnation in Jesus. The New Testament account speaks both of the continuity between Jesus and others and of the difference. Process thought can do that also.

The New Testament passage that played the largest role in the early church in shaping the understanding of the incarnation is found in the first chapter of the gospel according to John. Some scholars believe that what is here identified as Logos had earlier been called, in the language of Paul, among others, Sophia. Would that this naming had been kept! However, I will stay with "Logos" for our present purposes.

According to John 1, from eternity a divine reason grounded order and meaning in the world. According to Whitehead, a divine envisagement provides order and novelty in the world. Whitehead calls it the "primordial nature" of God. According to the gospel, nothing was created apart from the Logos. According to Whitehead, nothing comes into being apart from the primordial nature. According to the gospel, this relationship is especially manifested in life and in mental activity as the light that enlightens all people. The same statement describes reality as explained by Whitehead.

John does not explicitly say that the life and light expressive of the working of the Logos are immanent, but surely that is the most natural interpretation. For Whitehead, life and light express the immanence of the primordial nature of God. When we move to specific statements about Jesus, these close parallels end. Although Whitehead makes some very positive statements about Jesus, he writes as a philosopher and not as a Christian believer. He does not talk about God's specific relationship to Jesus. However, let us see how John speaks of it and consider his formulations from a contemporary process perspective.

John makes two key statements about Jesus. The second is the most famous. John 1:14 asserts that the Logos became *carne* (flesh) and lived among us. The word "incarnation" derives from this verse. It means enfleshment. *Carne* has a range of meanings, but in this case it is generally, and rightly, understood to be a fully embodied human being. The verse can hardly mean that the Logos in its entirety was transformed into a single human being. The cosmic functions of the eternal Logos did not cease, but John understood the way the divine Logos was present in Jesus to be distinctive. This difference was very important.

The earlier formulation in John 1:9 may help us to understand how John thought both of the continuity and of the difference: "The true light which enlightens everyone was coming into the world." Clearly the true light, which is the Logos, was already functioning in the world before and apart from Jesus, enlightening everyone. The Stoics thought a spark of the divine Logos lived in every human being. John suggests something of this sort. Neither the Stoics nor John thought that this spark sufficed to make all people recognize or understand the truth. The light struggled with the darkness. Then in Jesus, John was convinced, the light burst through in full glory, expressed in the fullness of Jesus' very flesh, his fully embodied humanity. No one has ever seen God, but Jesus has made God known.

Today a Christian believer who adopts Whitehead's way of thinking must be wary of some of John's formulations. John wrote at a time when Jewish followers of Jesus were struggling against other Jews who rejected him. John belittled the extent of knowledge of God that these other Jews had from the shared scriptures. Nevertheless, as twenty-first-century Christians, we can join John in affirming that it is the fullness of incarnation of the light in Jesus through which we know God.

Through the incarnation of the light in Jesus, we also discern its presence in everyone. No one is without the life and light that is the divine presence in him or her. However much the darkness of sin and ignorance and prejudice might obscure that light, it does not quench it altogether. The reality and new possibilities of life and goodness are always there. Through Jesus we learn to approach each person in terms of the divine promise that works within them, rather than in terms of the distortions that too often seem to dominate human thought and action.

As Whiteheadians, we enthusiastically follow John yet another step. John distinguished living things and especially human beings from the inanimate world. But the Logos is at work there, too. No creation occurs apart from the Logos. Today the lines between the animate and the inanimate are blurred. We see more continuity than was visible when John wrote. John also saw one and the same divine reality creatively at work in all things. His was an incarnational vision. The tasks of preserving and developing that vision have never been more important than today.

I think that many process thinkers are open to the possibility that while ministering on Earth, Jesus, at times, did not choose to respond to God's initial aims for him. That is what makes him so distinctly human. Yet, clearly something about his life and death created a vast field of force that continues to draw people to him and his life.

Why was Jesus more receptive to God's aims than the rest of us?

The assumption underlying this question is that Jesus' distinctiveness lies primarily in the fullness with which he responded to God's aims for him. This is the view of a number of process Christologies. Other liberal Christologies have similar ideas, beginning with Schleiermacher. He thought that whereas God-consciousness plays some role in everyone, it was perfect in Jesus. In the Ritschlian tradition, some affirmed that the distinctiveness of Jesus lay in the perfection of his moral character.

My own approach has a different emphasis, but I want to give some response to the question posed in this way. I certainly believe that Jesus was far more receptive to God's aims than I am and that the vast majority of people are. To what can we attribute this greater-than-normal receptiveness?

As long as the question is just about a greater-than-normal receptiveness, I do not see it as requiring an answer. We assume considerable differences among people on many qualities. That some are more responsive to God's call than others is what we would expect. Indeed, we would expect a considerable variation. Perhaps genetic factors play a role, but I would rather emphasize human freedom. Nothing compels one to be responsive or resistant. That is the decision made moment by moment.

The rhetoric we use about Jesus, however, often singles him out in such an extreme way that this kind of answer may seem insufficient. Even for extreme differences, we have analogies. The difference between Mozart's musical abilities and mine are truly extreme. In the spiritual realm, I would say the same of Gautama Buddha's and mine, or of St. Francis' and mine. These people inspire awe and wonder. Genetically determined gifts may explain part of the difference, but at least in the moral and spiritual sphere, the answer is primarily in the way people exercise their freedom.

I mentioned that although I do believe that Jesus was wonderfully responsive to God's call, I do not think of this as an adequate way to talk about his uniqueness. He may not have been more responsive than Gautama or Francis. Some simple people of whom we have never heard may have also been extraordinarily responsive to God's call. Perhaps Jesus was the most responsive of all, but in itself I do not think that accounts for his distinctiveness.

To me, to focus on what Jesus was called to be and do is equally important. Let us suppose that he was called so to actualize the Jewish faith of his day that it could have an appeal and a relevance far beyond the Jewish community. It is clear that responding to that call was not what Gautama and Francis were about. Or perhaps Jesus was called to relate to God in such a way that others would be able to see in and through him what God is like. That is not what God called Gautama to do and be, and insofar as that would apply to Francis, it would be in a way derivative from what happened in Jesus.

Jesus would not have described his call in these ways. People are often unaware of deeper divine purposes. Jesus seems not to have had Gentiles in mind, except peripherally. The passages in John that emphasize seeing God in and through Jesus are unlikely to reflect Jesus' own thinking. I am inferring God's purposes from the future course of events, and of these Jesus was ignorant. Jesus understood his call to be to proclaim repentance in view of the imminence of the *basileia theou* (the kingdom, or commonwealth, of God). Responding to that call faithfully led him to crucifixion. It also led to an understanding of Judaism that opened its doors to Gentiles. In Paul's view, both Jews and Gentiles are to participate in Jesus' faithfulness, which now defines the righteousness of God.

The distinctiveness of the call would have made very little difference had Jesus not been extraordinarily responsive. Even if we decided that Gautama and Francis responded equally well to the call of God, Jesus would remain uniquely important to us and authoritative for us. Jesus' faithfulness had historical effects very different from the faithfulness of Gautama and Francis.

When we attend to the nature of the call to which Jesus responded so well, the question of the special situation of Jesus makes a lot of sense. First of all, Jesus was a Jew. Only a Jew, a very devout Jew, could have heard and responded to the kind of call that came to Jesus. He lived in Galilee, and the kind of Judaism he received was probably the only kind that could have led him to teach and act as he did. Whitehead suggests that the powerlessness of the Galilean Jews enabled them to think more radically about the ideal life than was possible for persons who had some practical control over public affairs. In Jesus' day, Judaism was already attractive to many Gentiles, so that the changes in Jewish teaching that derived indirectly from him sufficed to open the doors of the communities of his followers to the full participation of many Gentiles.

In no way do we intend to minimize the mystery of Jesus' faithfulness. We only want to say that the call that came to him, and the vast effects in human history of his responsiveness, were possible only in the very specific historical circumstances of that time. The ideal for Christians today is to be as faithful to God's call to us as Jesus was to his call in his day. Even if we fulfill that calling in concrete ways, we would still not be very much like Jesus. The effects of our faithfulness would not be similar to his.

I have tried to move the discussion into another dimension as well. My proposals are controversial among process thinkers, and I acknowledge that they are speculative. I do not apologize for that, since I believe in speculating, that is, in proposing hypotheses and working out their implications. I do acknowledge that the evidence for this speculation is limited. Still, I will sketch my arguments again. I have worked them out more fully in *Christ in a Pluralistic Age*.

These are Whiteheadian speculations, but probably not ones with which Whitehead would have been particularly pleased. That is, they employ Whitehead's analysis of actual occasions but do so for purposes that express very specific Christian interests. I want to see how far I can go toward making sense of the beliefs of early Christians about Jesus' relation to God.

My speculation is that in different occasions of human experience, the various prehensions that make up an occasion are related to one another in diverse ways. In most of us Westerners, at least, the most determinative prehension is that of our personal past. I inherit from that past all sorts of desires and anxieties and deep-seated habits. I interpret other prehensions from this point of view. Some of them appear threatening, others comforting. I allow some to make major contributions to my experience in each moment and I minimize others. The "I" that does this is constituted by the prehension of my personal past.

I also experience a prehension of God. This is God's call. I experience this call as coming from another. It, too, may be threatening or comforting. I admit it into my experience more or less, and I conform to it more or less.

Having described this normal structure of experience, I judge that it does not characterize everyone all the time. It does not characterize very small children. It does not characterize enlightened Buddhists. It does not characterize theistic mystics. I believe that, during much of his ministry, it did not characterize Jesus.

In every moment, what I would call "me" is actually a dominant center in a continuous succession of momentary experiences. "I" am constituted anew every moment by the successive impinging of my personal past on this new occasion. The initial aim from God is also present in this moment, but I experience it as "other"–something about which I need to make a decision. In the case of Jesus, my argument is that God was so fully prehended by Jesus, that is, so constitutively present, that Jesus did not experience God as other. In each moment of his existence, the I of Jesus was *jointly* constituted by his personal past *and* his prehension of God, such that Jesus did not feel God as an other about which a decision needed to be made. God's presence and the influence of the past together formed the perspective from which Jesus constituted himself–his "I"–from moment to moment.

This speculation brings a process Christology somewhat into line with the Christologies of the early church. These sought to affirm the integral union of the human and the Divine in Jesus. They did so in terms of substance, in ways closed to process thinkers. In the process approach, it is necessary to ask the question of the structure of Jesus' existence and the role that God played in it moment by moment. Whereas some of Jesus' sayings suggest that he felt free to speak for God, at other times he experienced himself as sharply separated from God. The speculation I have offered applies only to the former times. It undergirds the idea that Jesus' sayings have peculiar authority. But, of course, they remain thoroughly historically and culturally conditioned.

What is the process view of redemption?

If process theology does not address the topic of redemption, broadly conceived, it is hardly a theology at all! To respond to this challenge, we must address two distinct questions. First, is the word "redemption" commonly used by process theologians? I have not thematically treated it in my writings, nor have I done research to see where "redemption" is thematically discussed by other process theologians. However, a quick check assures me that Marjorie Suchocki has used the word systematically in her book, *The End of Evil.*

More important is the question whether the Christian concerns to which the word "redemption" points are more widely pervasive within process theology. I think they are. Consider my *Christ in a Pluralistic Age.* Although the word appears rarely and almost incidentally, I would claim that "redemption," broadly understood, is central to the whole book. This claim depends on the belief that "redemption" has multiple meanings that can be discussed under multiple headings.

The first part of the book deals chiefly with "creative transformation." I take that to be fundamental to what Christ is doing in the world as the incarnation of God. The second part of the book deals with Jesus' role in this process of creative transformation. Part three explores what we can and should hope for, that is, in what way can we and the world of which we are a part be creatively transformed? I could easily use the word "redemption" to formulate this question.

It would be unfortunate if it were felt that lack of commitment to the word "redemption" were a sign of departure from the New

Testament. A quick check of a concordance indicates that "redemption" is used only occasionally in the Bible (the Greek noun apolytrōsis occurs ten times in the New Testament–Lk. 21:28; Rom. 3:24; 8:23; 1 Cor. 1:30; Eph. 1:7, 14; 4:30; Col. 1:14; Heb. 9:15; 11:35; the verb exagorazō four times–Gal. 3:13; 4:5; Eph. 5:16; Col. 4:5; the verb lytroō three times–Lk. 24:21; Titus 2:14; 1 Pet. 1:18; the noun lytrōsis three times–Lk. 1:68; 2:38; Heb. 9:12; the noun lytrōtēs once–Acts 7:35). Since I have recently published a commentary on Romans, with David Lull, a process New Testament scholar, I will comment on Paul's use of the word in that important letter. My concordance finds two uses: Romans 3:24 and 8:23. Both are in passages with which we wrestled very seriously.

I find it interesting to see how we dealt with redemption in these two passages. In the second passage, the redemption is of the body. For Paul this is the final stage of our hoped-for resurrection. We described this as a transformation of the physical body into a spiritual body. This connects it to Paul's account elsewhere of the resurrection of Jesus and what that leads us to anticipate (1 Cor. 15:42–44).

Most Christians, however, are concerned with the other passage in Romans where the word is used. This passage has been the basis for much thinking about how we are redeemed by Jesus' sacrifice. Because of its great impact on the thinking of the church, we spent a good deal of time on Romans 3:23–25a. Lull developed a translation of the Greek text quite different from the Revised Standard Version– one that we believe is more literal. I will not spell out the reasons for all the changes here but simply say that many of them are based on recent textual scholarship. Our translation is as follows.

> The reason why God's righteousness is for all who are faithful is that there is no distinction among people. For all have sinned and fallen short of God's glory, so that all are justified by God's grace as a gift through the liberation effected by Christ Jesus. God presented Christ Jesus as an act of conciliation through [and because of] Jesus' faithfulness even to death. God did this to show God's righteousness. (Rom. 3:23–25a)

You will notice that we did not use the English word "redemption" in this translation. The Greek word typically translated as "redemption" is used with respect to a payment made for the freeing of a slave. The focus here is on our being made free by Jesus' faithfulness, even to death. We thought this came through more clearly in the English with the word "liberation." But as long as the reader hears in "redeem" the idea of making free, we are happy with the word "redemption."

Our view is that Paul did not connect this sacrificial death of Jesus with the Jewish Day of Atonement. He does not show signs of having this model in mind anywhere else in his writings. This model leads to the idea that God plays the role of the priest and Jesus the role of the animal that is sacrificed. Since we do not like the theology based on that image—that is, the idea of God sacrificing Jesus—we may be accused of reading our preferred ideas into the text. However, it is our genuine conviction, being as objective as we can, that our translation is closer to Paul's meaning.

I have spent more time on this passage because for some Christians the idea of "redemption" is closely associated with that of an atonement effected by God through sacrificing Jesus. If someone is looking for this doctrine in process theology, she or he is likely to be disappointed. It does not fit with the process idea of God. We think it does not fit with the idea of God taught by Jesus or by Paul.

Lull and I have concluded that Paul's central idea is that when we participate in the faithfulness of Jesus, sharing in his suffering and death, God views us in light of that participation and treats us as righteous despite our continuing sinfulness. In the end we will be glorified as Jesus was glorified in resurrection, and even our bodies will be transformed. If this is what one means by redemption, then redemption was certainly central for Paul, even though the word is not prominent in his writings.

Jesus' central message was about the coming of God's *basileia* (commonwealth). Preparing for that through repentance was his call. Already, there and then, those who heard him could follow him into living in terms of that new order rather than the expectations and requirements of the Roman Empire. Jesus did not speak of "redemption," but in a broad sense that was certainly the meaning of his proclamation.

Neither Jesus nor Paul expressed an idea of God's sacrificing Jesus to atone for human sins or to ransom us from the devil's power. Those ideas do have some foothold in the Bible. Process theologians in general prefer the theologies of Jesus and Paul.

I rehearse this to remind us that already in the New Testament, the good news takes a variety of forms. In general, the term "redemption" is not prominent either in the New Testament or in process theology. If we use it in a broad way to identify the promise of change that Jesus and Paul announced in different ways, then it is indeed at the heart of Christian theology. Process theology is then about redemption.

Process theologians want to make the promise of change as real and as realistic as possible for twenty-first-century people. Many theologians have highlighted "liberation" as the best name for this change today. Most process theologians have generally favored this language as well. Some of us think that "creative transformation" is a helpful and fruitful way to name what we receive from God and hope for in the future. We seek a creative transformation of personal lives, or social structures, and of the global situation. For some of us, the salvation of humanity and other creatures from the self-destruction in which we are now engaged is the most important "redemption" of all. When I write about a new economic order, I consider myself to be discussing "redemption."

Whitehead taught us to rejoice in the way that God creatively transforms all that we are, moment by moment, into a part of God's own life. Through that transformation our lives become everlasting. For him this is what saves us from meaninglessness. Suchocki's thinking about redemption deals mostly with what we become in God. Some of us are also interested in another creative transformation, one that may take place at death, into a new ongoing life. Others think it best not to introduce this topic into Christian theology. None of us want to encourage preoccupation with a future life in another sphere or dimension.

No one doctrine of redemption follows necessarily and universally for all process theologians. We have varied ideas and emphases, just as one finds variety also in the New Testament. For the most part our ideas are complementary rather than contradictory of one another. That does not mean that we all agree. We hope that the diversity of opinions about redemption will keep process theology moving and developing in a fruitful direction.

How does process theology answer the question of bodily resurrection?

The resurrection is a powerful symbol, and liberal churches treat it primarily as such. It is a symbol of victory over loss and defeat. The crucifixion of Jesus seemed to be a final defeat, but out of it came a movement that has profoundly affected the course of history and to which many of us look for the meaning and purpose of life. Some of us can testify to our own experiences of apparent hopelessness that gave way to new possibilities. When one is near despair, the symbol of resurrection can be a profoundly important one.

This symbol can function without regard to what happened to either the body or the soul of Jesus. For many liberal Christians, this suffices. For them further questions about just what actually happened are inappropriate. At the ultimate level, I incline to support this view. Jesus called us to live from the *basileia theou,* the divine commonwealth that contrasts sharply with every existent social order. One can do that without knowing anything more about what happened to Jesus. Jesus' resurrection does mean at least this much: What from a worldly perspective seems impractical, even impossible, can happen and sometimes does happen.

Nevertheless, at a penultimate level, these questions remain important. I am haunted by Paul's words in 1 Corinthians 15:19: "If for this life only we have hoped in Christ, we are of all people the most to be pitied." It reminds me of a somewhat analogous statement of Whitehead near the end of the chapter on "Religion and Science" in *Science and the Modern World.* There he states that, apart from the religious vision, "human life is a flash of occasional enjoyments lighting up a mass of pain and misery, a bagatelle of transient experience" (192).

I do not think Paul is quite right, but I still take him seriously. For him, Jesus' rising from the dead was the foretaste of a glorious destiny. What is the meaning of Christian hope if specific hopes are not underlain by an ultimate confidence? What is the basis of that confidence if it is not, as with Paul, an actual transformation of the historical figure Jesus?

Even for Paul, the answers here could be qualified. His belief in the resurrection in general did not depend on Jesus' resurrection. He was already a Pharisee. Although he accepted the accounts of Jesus appearing to the apostles after his death as being resurrection appearances, they did not provide the model for the resurrection for which all hunger. This was not the ability to appear to living people after death. It was instead a glorious transformation into a spiritual body. His own vision on the road to Damascus was of the glorified Jesus in heaven. The fullest and clearest account of what this means for believers is given in Romans 8. It seems there that the transformation into glory is the destiny of the whole created order.

If this means that the whole created order will cease to exist and will be superseded by this glory, I am not able to follow. But it may not mean that. In 1 Corinthians 15, Paul speaks of a transformation from a physical body to a spiritual body. Did he mean that the physical body ceases to exist when the spiritual body is raised? In that case, the tomb must have been empty, but Paul never mentions an empty tomb. We will not have to break much with Paul if we suppose that the person who once existed as a physical body now exists as a spiritual one. The physical body is dead and behaves as physical things do. The spiritual body is alive and behaves as spiritual things do.

If we pursue this line of thinking, it turns out that Whitehead's vision of how all events are included and transformed in the consequent nature of God is not so far removed from the glorification of the cosmos anticipated by Paul. We can say that believers, all people, and all things are resurrected to a glory that we share with the Jesus whom Paul saw on the road to Damascus.

I agree with Whitehead that this is of critical importance. Apart from God, all things are ephemeral. No sooner is a value realized than it passes. For a little while it lingers on in human memory, but that is also soon gone. When this is understood to be the whole story, more than one response is still possible. One is expressed in the proverb "Eat, drink, and be merry, for tomorrow you may die," which derives from the King James Version of Ecclesiastes 8:15 and Isaiah 22:13. In other words, seize what pleasure you can moment by moment. The truth, we all know, is that making ultimate the sorts of pleasures possible in this context does not produce much happiness.

Another response is the Buddhist one. When one fully realizes the transience of all things, one gives up the effort to find or impose meaning. One accepts what happens as it happens, whatever it is. One thereby achieves wisdom because of one's freedom from all distorting presuppositions. One becomes compassionate because one's personal hopes and fears no longer block one's openness to others.

This is a beautiful goal, rarely attained in full, but beneficial even in partial realizations. It can be appreciated by those of us shaped by the Abrahamic traditions, but it can be fully appropriated only by giving up what is central to our tradition. We seek an altered world. We bring norms of justice and community to bear in judging this world, and we seek to commit ourselves accordingly. This process of evaluation and commitment is threatened when we view the transitoriness of things as being the whole story. The belief that it is not the whole story, that the ephemeral world is transformed in God, can ground continued evaluation and commitment within the historical process.

From a Whiteheadian perspective, I have no difficulty in believing that Jesus has been glorified in this way and that this knowledge undergirds those who follow him. But did Jesus have ongoing experiences after he died on the cross? Does that matter? The New Testament accounts of the resurrection appearance certainly answer this question in the affirmative. The resurrected Jesus interacted with his disciples. His disciples were transformed from fear and despair to confidence and action.

Is there any factual basis for these stories? If not, who invented them? Conscious invention overall seems unlikely, since that would not suffice to explain the new confidence of the apostles. But if there were actual events, what was their nature? Were they convincing hallucinations? Or were they actual auditions and visions? Does it matter?

The changes in the apostles could be explained by either. In either case, they would judge that Jesus was alive again. This would mean that God had raised him and that they were called to proclaim his resurrection and to continue his proclamation. This would explain the historical phenomena. But it would do so in a way that was quite opposite from the understanding of those who were involved.

Another explanation is that the apostles had authentic experience of the risen Jesus. Unfortunately, this is too often associated with "ghosts," which are usually understood quite negatively. Many convincing stories come from recently deceased persons appearing to their loved ones and communicating with them. Unless one assumes that this is impossible, the most natural interpretation of the New Testament accounts is in these terms. If one accepts that such things happen, then one assumes that personal existence does not end with death. Belief that Jesus appeared after his death confirms this general belief in personal survival of some sort.

That belief, of course, also has religious importance. But clearly the reasoning is circular. If one believes in survival after death and that, at least for a short time, some of those who have died appear to those they have left behind, then that person will be very likely to interpret the Easter stories in this way, as do I. If one does not believe in personal survival or the possibility of communication, one will not do so.

Precisely because the tradition hands down so many somewhat similar stories, the special importance of these appearances of one who has recently died depends on who it is that reappears. Because Jesus appeared to the apostles, their shattered belief that he was the anointed one for whom Israel hoped was renewed. Recollection of his words and deeds became a matter of greatest importance to them. They were now ready to accept his lordship and to give themselves without limit to his cause.

Such an understanding by no means answers all our questions. On the contrary, it opens the way to many and diverse speculations. It is very important for Christians not to attach primary importance to such questions. But it is perfectly legitimate to wonder about them and to form opinions about them. Whitehead's conceptuality opens the door to multiple possibilities without settling the decision among them. One who judges that the apostles hallucinated is not rendered thereby a less faithful disciple. One who judges that the tomb was emptied by a strictly supernatural act of God is not thereby a better Christian. The critical issue is our discipleship, not our opinions on such matters.

Does it make sense to say that Jesus is really present in the eucharist?

This idea has been very important in the history of Christianity. The eucharist is central to Roman Catholicism to this day. It is understood and affirmed that the bread and wine in some sense become the body and blood of Jesus. Obviously, no one means that the sensible qualities of the bread and wine disappear to be replaced by those of human flesh and blood. The central point is that when the elements are consecrated, the event of Jesus' sharing a meal with his disciples, suffering death on the cross, and rising again becomes present and real. This was explained in Aristotelian terms as a change of the substance of the bread and wine into the substance of the body and blood of Jesus without any change in the attributes or sensory qualities.

The Reformers broke with this Aristotelian account. Lutherans argued that the substance of Jesus became present in the sacrament without replacing the substance of the bread and wine. They contrasted this consubstantiation to the Catholic transubstantiation. Calvinists gave up the language of substance but insisted all the same on the "real presence." This was the heart of the matter for all three.

In the absence of a philosophical account of the real presence, many Calvinists were influenced by the dominant mind-set of the time. The only thing that could be really present, from this point of view, was the present. The present contains not only sense experience of the external world but also memory of the past. In the New Testament account of the Lord's supper, Jesus tells his disciples to share bread and wine in memory of him. Hence the real presence could be understood to mean Jesus' presence to us through our conscious memory or recollection of his last supper, his death, and his rising to new life.

This involved a shift of the understanding of Jesus' presence from a strong emphasis on objectivity to an almost pure subjectivity. Whereas Catholics and Lutherans taught that Jesus was present in the bread and wine, whatever subjective state participants were in, this tendency in the churches influenced by Calvin implied that Jesus' presence is proportional to the vividness with which he is recalled. The purpose of observing the sacrament is to increase the power of this memory.

Process thought provides a third option. In a process perspective, the whole past is really present quite apart from whether it is remembered in any conscious way. That means that the events emphasized in the eucharist are influential among all people everywhere at all times, just as are all other past events. Even if people have never heard the Christian story, those past events play some role in their present unconscious experience. Of course, much of the time this presence is trivial with many people.

Certain past events have a far greater role in constituting the present than others. One can trace this importance through the course of history. The enlightenment of Gautama has had an enormous influence through his disciples and their teaching. It has established an ideal that influences whole cultures. It has been studied and emulated. Most of this influence does not depend on the conscious interests and memories of a person in a Buddhist culture at any given time. When one is engaged in meditation, the influence, or the real presence, of Gautama is certainly heightened.

Jesus' influence in Christendom, but even far beyond Christendom, has also been enormous. It has been mediated in many ways, but perhaps the strongest and most consistent has been through the regular observance of the eucharist in tens of thousands of communities. The real, causal presence does not depend on the state of consciousness of those who are influenced. Placing oneself in the context of a worshiping community that is celebrating the eucharist greatly heightens that objective influence. The role of those past events in constituting the present experience is enhanced. Jesus is really present.

In this process account, the real presence is not focused narrowly on the bread and wine, as in the major tradition. Jesus is really present in the whole event, but especially in the experiences of those persons who participate. In this respect, the process account resembles the account of those who emphasize memory as the key element. It differs in that the real presence of Jesus does not depend on conscious memory. Such memory is a valuable contributor to the effectiveness of the real presence, but such memory is as much a result of the real presence as its cause.

Process thought also explains the importance for Christians of the real presence. In Whitehead's account, physical feelings function in the conformal stage of concrescence. That is, the becoming occasion conforms to those aspects of the past that it prehends. If the prehension of Jesus plays a significant role in the concrescence of the new occasion, there will be significant conformation to what is prehended. For Christians, conformation to Jesus is of highest importance.

We may ask, Does this explanation make a difference? I think it does. It is a difference typical of the one that the process approach makes in theology more broadly. When this kind of explanation is not available, the choice tends to be between supernatural explanations and reductive ones. The justification for the supernatural explanation is that the lived experience implies more than the reductive account allows. The justification for the reductive account is that the supernaturalist explanation seems incredible and tends toward magical thinking. Process theology seeks to do justice to the lived experience of the believing participant in the eucharist without proposing an incredible explanation.

Obviously, when the real presence is understood in this way, it is not limited to the eucharist. This may be the most effective way to heighten the reality of the presence of those past events it celebrates, but it is not the only way. Jesus can be effectively present in nonsacramental churches and in the nonsacramental activities of all churches.

Furthermore, this account does not minimize the value of the experience of persons in other religious traditions. Christians find the presence of Jesus in their lives to be of great value. This does not exclude the fact that the presence of Gautama is of great value in the lives of Buddhists. Nor does it imply that the only source of supremely valuable experiences is the presence of the past. We need to be as open as possible to the way people in other traditions understand their experiences and seek to understand those different experiences as accurately as possible. None of this will detract from the joy that Christians feel over the presence of Jesus in their lives.

7

The Problem of Evil

From time to time, public events of such horrific magnitude occur that people are driven to ask why God allows them. They may know in a general way that a good many theologians have taught that God grants us freedom and that God's purposes in creating us would not be fulfilled if God took that freedom away from us too easily. We would not learn to take responsibility for our own actions. When historical evil rises to really terrible levels, this argument ceases to seem adequate. To take away Hitler's freedom would seem a minor price to pay if it would save millions of Jewish lives. To take away Saddam Hussein's freedom, if thereby the horrendous suffering of the Iraqi people could have been avoided as well as the international crisis caused by his intransigence and the American conquest of Iraq, would seem a small price indeed in comparison with the likely gain. Why does God sit idly by?

Process theologians believe this question is beyond answer as long as we leave the idea of God's omnipotence intact. Those who believe they can maintain God's omnipotence by arguing for God's self-limitation often think they have solved the problem. In their view, God could control everything, but from the beginning God chose to limit God's role in the world. They conclude that God judged that it would be better to leave space for creaturely freedom and that God never goes back on this decision.

Several problems beset this position. First, we can easily think of a better decision the omnipotent God could have made. God could have decided to make space for creaturely freedom within limits. This is what sensible parents do for their children. They let their children make more and more of their own decisions as they grow older, but these parents are prepared to intervene to prevent their children from seriously harming themselves and others. We would arrest a parent who acted in the way this "self-limited God" is said to act. Presumably, an omnipotent God could have made a decision more like that of a good parent and acted upon it with infinite wisdom.

Second, if this decision of God means that God is not involved in human actions, the whole idea of God's action in history is undercut. Indeed, it is hard to reconcile a doctrine of the incarnation with this decision. On the other hand, the problem arises that once any exception is allowed, the question arises why there are not others.

We do have an alternative here. Historically, theologians have made a great deal of God's persuasive work with human beings in the world. The divine decision not to interfere might leave open the possibility that God would work persuasively but not coercively. God's activity in history, even the incarnation, could be understood on this basis.

Even so, the first question remains. Why, in extreme cases, when so much is at stake, does God not intervene forcefully to prevent extreme forms of evil? If God has the power to do so and refrains, just to be faithful to an unwise decision made long ago, we find it hard to admire such a foolishly stubborn God and even harder to love that God.

The underlying premise of all of this is divine omnipotence. Because people suppose that God can do anything, they marvel that such terrible things happen. Classically, the situation was much worse. To many Christians, omnipotence meant not only that God could act in any way but also that, in fact, God did act in just the way that events actually transpired. If God has all the power, they reasoned, whatever happens is ultimately what God wills to happen. Then God did not simply sit idly by while Hitler and Saddam committed their atrocities. God willed those atrocities. That makes it even harder to love God! The doctrine of divine self-limitation was invented to reduce the contradiction between the reality of overwhelming evil and the teaching that God is love.

Process theology flatly rejects the idea of omnipotence that underlies all this discussion. Some process theologians redefine omnipotence as ideal power rather than all-controlling power, and then explain it in quite a different way. Others just reject the doctrine of omnipotence as such. We believe that God is very powerful but that God's power is not the sort of power envisaged by those who ask these questions about God and give these answers.

In process theology, God persuades and does not coerce. This is not simply a decision that could be reversed at any time so that we are led to wonder why God has not intervened coercively. On the contrary, we believe that the God we know in Jesus Christ empowers, gives freedom, and guides. God is the power that makes for life, for healing, and for growth. God is the power through which understanding and wisdom arise. God is the power by virtue of which humans have an awareness of better and worse. God is the power behind loving relations among people. Without this power we would not exist at all. This power brought us into being through millions of years of evolution. We have no reason to think that this method was arbitrarily chosen. Since divine power is persuasive and since creatures are typically resistant, it takes millions of years to bring such creatures into existence.

How we use the expanded freedom that comes with our humanness is a matter of great import. God calls us to use it with a view to the wider good, but we often resist. The vast expansion of technological power over nature to which we have come renders us capable of ever greater evil. God's persuasive work becomes ever more important. Indeed, divine persuasion is our only basis for historical hope. But it guarantees nothing.

God can only work in the concrete situations of the world. Those situations, which are often shaped extensively by our sinful decisions "tie God's hands." God can bring some novelty, some healing, some transformation to any situation if we allow that to happen. But the novelty, healing, and transformation God can bring are always closely tied to the specificity of the situation.

God does not stand by and watch Hitler and Saddam and others commit atrocities. God calls for very different behavior, but many throughout history have hardened their hearts. Sadly, many do so today. Many who sensitively deplore every injury and death that befalls American troops seem unable to extend equal concern to the Iraqi people. As Jesus made very clear, God calls us toward the expansion of our sympathy and toward actions that express that expansion. If we continue to refuse that call even as our world grows smaller, the consequences will be more and more catastrophic.

Some Christians are shocked by our denial to God of controlling power. They suppose that the idea of God's almighty power is central to the biblical vision. But they are mistaken. Given the many biblical authors who wrote over a long period of time, one must acknowledge that the Bible offers many views of divine power. The idea that God is almighty comes to us mainly through the decision of translators to replace one of the proper names for God, El Shaddai, with "God Almighty." This is a quite arbitrary replacement. Nothing in the Bible warrants it.

Process theologians believe that God's power is revealed in and through Jesus. We believe that Paul understood it well. If so, the idea that God's power is controlling is quite discordant. God's power is the power of love.

Process theologians believe God acts in another way—by receiving creatures into the divine life. Traditionally, God was thought to be impassive, that is, unaffected by what happens in the world. The biblical God and the God of process theology is infinitely sensitive to what happens. We believe that a God is revealed in Christ who is always present with us, who suffers with us in our sufferings, and who rejoices with us in our joys. God was not standing by while millions of Jews were exterminated by Nazis. God was with them in the camps, experiencing their tortures with them, and dying with them in the gas chambers. The power to be with us in this way is a very great power. In its ideal form it is uniquely divine power.

How does process theology explain natural evils?

As in so many respects, process thought turns questions of this sort upside down. Generally, people have explained evil in the human world by focusing on sin as a characteristic of human beings. Then they have asked how to explain natural evil. The classical answer was that this, too, is the consequence of human sin. Process theologians believe that in the context of a world that existed for billions of years before human beings came along, that answer is absurd. Even if we restrict the problem of evil to sentient beings, we must recognize that for hundreds of millions of years creatures have suffered at each other's hands and as a result of natural disasters that have nothing to do with human beings. It is better to develop an understanding of God and the world that fits with what we know of this long evolutionary process than to start with one that fits only the human situation.

One way of relating God and the world is what we call Deism. In this view God brought the world into being and established the laws by which it would operate and then left it to itself. If we think this way, we will wonder whether the laws God established are the best possible. They allow for so much suffering. One wonders also why the initial creative act did not produce a world that included more advanced beings. The initiation of our world through the Big Bang and billions of years of development seems odd.

What makes it odd, of course, is the presupposition that God is all-powerful, so that God could have created in a quite different way. All that we really know is that the world came into being through this very lengthy process in a generally law-abiding way. Many people see no reason to bring God into the picture at all. An omnipotent God fits with this picture very poorly.

What roles might God be seen as playing here? If we accept the now orthodox idea of the Big Bang, it is possible to think that God caused it. Just how to think of that depends on how we think of the Big Bang, and on this there is no consensus. My preference is to think of an infinite "empty" space in Whitehead's sense, that is, a space filled with tiny bursts of energy but lacking in any enduring objects such as what we now call "particles." The beginning of our universe is the coming into being of such particles. For reasons beyond my scientific understanding, this entrance of particles in the space-filled world caused a great explosion. Without this, nothing of significant value would ever have emerged. We may see a role for God in this coming to be of a new order of reality.

A second role can be attributed to God. Scientists marvel at the physical constants that govern the process once it is initiated. If any one or several of these physical constants had been different, life could never have come into being. In other words, they seem to be geared to the production of higher values. Since the constants are presupposed by all events and cannot be seen as resulting from them, it is easy to seek a cause beyond the flux of events. Such a cause may well be thought of as God.

From this point on, many think of the further development of reality as the mechanical working out of the impulses generated in the initial explosion following the constants primordially established. In that case the world has no further role for God. Some think that this mechanistic explanation ceases to work with the emergence of human freedom. At that point one can again relate God to the world as calling for the right use of freedom.

Following Whitehead, process thinkers reject this picture. We think that the individual entities that made up the world even before the Big Bang and still populate empty space are not wholly determined in a mechanistic way. They are acts, growing out of the past but not wholly determined by that past. They, too, are subject to God's persuasion, although the element of persuadability may be vanishingly small. We suspect that God had been luring the occasions in empty space to constitute particles long before this actually happened. We think this persuasive process has continued from that time to this, bringing more complex creatures into being. These more complex beings are more subject to God's persuasive activity, although, like the simpler ones, what they become moment by moment is chiefly determined by their situation.

Does this run contrary to evidence? We do not think so. The constants make possible the evolution of more complex living beings. Whether these come into being, and if so, what form they take, does not seem to be preestablished. Chance and purpose have a role to play. A place appears to see God at work in the course of events.

Is the claim that God is at work compatible with the natural evils that abound in the process of cosmic expansion? I think so. God's persuasive work with individual entities has no effect on the movements of the stars. It has negligible effect on the falling of a stone. It is trivial with most electronic occasions. To effect the breakthroughs so important in cosmic history took a lot of luring! Even with living things, God's persuasion does not work to limit their mutual destructiveness. If a lion is chasing a gazelle, I assume that God is encouraging the gazelle to escape and the lion to capture and kill it. Predation is part of the process that brings into being more complex creatures capable of greater enjoyment.

God has a great deal to do with evolutionary process in that apart from the aim of living beings "to live, to live well, and to live better," this process would not have occurred. I believe, following Whitehead, that God lures the creatures in this direction. As more complex creatures with richer experience emerge, these creatures experience not only more enjoyment but also more suffering. The creatures impose such suffering on one another, and some suffering also results from external causes. To reduce suffering would be to reduce value as well. God's aim seems to be the increase of value even at great cost in suffering.

This did not change abruptly with the evolutionary emergence of our human ancestors. They related to one another and to other creatures much as other animals did. I believe that they suffered more and had greater enjoyment than any other species. They also developed far more complex ways of relating and thinking about their relations. This opened the door to a much larger role for God in their lives. For the first time, creatures could envision and evaluate the suffering they caused. God could lure them away from some of the activities that caused unnecessary suffering. God could lure them toward ways of relating to each other that brought comfort and joy, and even, eventually, of relating to strangers. But humans could also resist this calling.

In this picture one can see that although human sin is an important reason for evil at the human level, it is certainly not the only reason. The reasons for mutual destructiveness among other animals do not cease to operate among humans. In Whitehead's language, "life is robbery." (*Process and Reality*, 105). Creatures cannot continue to live without destroying others. Cooperation is extremely important even to survival, but competition is also inescapable. The evil that occurs among all living creatures continues with human beings and is exacerbated by their superior powers and emerging self-consciousness.

Critics of process theology assert that "our" God is too weak to be worthy of devotion. We certainly agree that God does not achieve divine purposes by forcing the world to conform. God's power is not of that sort. God always works with the world as it is, calling it to realize emerging possibilities. When the entities making up the world had minuscule capacity to respond, it took a very long time, by human time scales, to effect the needed changes. As God's work brought forth creatures with greater capacity to respond, change occurred more rapidly. With human beings, a whole new range of possibility came into being. The God who brought order out of chaos, life out of the inanimate, consciousness out of the unconscious, and love out of a world that knew no such relationship is not weak, in my view. This God calls me moment by moment to enjoyment, to truth, and to love. The call is also the empowerment to respond. That is a power far greater than the power to push me around and force me to conform. It is also the power revealed in Jesus.

What are your views on sin and evil? I wouldn't posit a literal existence for the devil, but I have the sense that there's something agentlike about evil that seems unaccounted for by process theology.

Let me say at the outset that I do not believe anyone, certainly including process theologians, has ever provided a fully adequate account of sin and evil. Most emphatically, this short response will not provide that.

I believe that our rapid depletion of resources and pollution of the environment are evils. I participate in these evils. Is that sin? In my view, it is sin when I participate more fully in them than I need to in order to accomplish positive goals. That is, sometimes I judge that driving the car or taking a trip by air, despite the use of scarce resources involved, is the right decision given all the relevant considerations. This does not mean my decision and ensuing actions cease to participate in evil. At other times I engage in waste knowingly, aware that I could do better. I consider that I am then sinning.

I am supposing that the initial aim in this latter case draws me toward avoiding waste. The questioner asks why, if God calls me to avoid waste and I know it, I still act wastefully. Is this sheer perversity?

Of course, it might be. I might be angry with God and simply want to flout God's call. Far more often I experience multiple pulls. I yield to laziness, established habits, a prideful judgment that I should be exempt from such petty considerations, or I just choose what is more pleasant. I do not understand this as either ignorance or perversity. Of course, my choice is not an example of a terrible sin. Nevertheless, repeatedly missing the mark of God's call in small matters like this affects our general sensitivity to that call and contributes to larger failures in our lives.

I want to make it clear that the systemic evil of degrading the Earth in our current situation is not primarily the result of individual sins of unnecessary wastefulness by those who know they are falling short of the ideal. The systemic evil results from our industrial-economic system. This system came into being out of a great mixture of motives. Some of them were narrowly selfish, and some of the decisions people made in the process were no doubt sinful. But not all. Some people rightly saw that the development of this system brought prosperity to nations and eventually to most of their people. Many were fully unaware of the ecological consequences. Even those who were aware considered that, for the most part, the gains of this system outweighed the losses.

I guess that in some instances individuals made decisions with some vague awareness that they were shutting out relevant considerations. Since I believe that to some extent we all miss the mark or fail to fully actualize the initial aim, I do not exclude sin as a causal element in the establishment of this system. My point is only that to explain the rise to dominance of this system primarily in terms of sin is extremely misleading. The evil results from a mixture of good intentions, ignorance, and sin. It is also profoundly brought about by the power of the past in each moment of human experience.

This last point requires unpacking. I believe that the power of the past is an important part of what makes evil seem "agentlike." The past has the dominant power to shape the present. The "many" that become "one" in each occasion are primarily past events. Once a system is established, it comes to seem self-evident and gains enormous support through its institutions. For example, at the time this industrial-capitalist system arose, it had little support in the university. Now it shapes much of what goes on there and exercises enormous influence. Anyone socialized by the dominant university culture will support the now-dominant system. This socialization into acceptance of the now-dominant system is, from my perspective, an evil. It has a demonic character. That is, the objective power of the system is far more determinative of the evil that transpires than are the sins or virtues of individuals. Even though most people are chiefly formed by the dominant attitudes of the societies in which they live, this does not mean that they are especially sinful. Most are genuinely persuaded of the validity of theories that support much of the destruction going on in our society. Mistaken beliefs, honestly held, play an enormous role in generating evil. On the other hand, I do believe that many people today have some awareness of a call to reject these beliefs, adopt others, change their personal habits, and try to change the system as well. People respond to this call more or less fully.

A major cause of historical evil is communal feeling. Such feeling is in itself a great good. We are members one of another and have special obligations to those to whom we are most closely related by blood, neighborhood, or other ties. It is good and important that most of us are willing to make some sacrifices for the sake of the communities of which we are a part.

But this great good is also the source of much of the evil in the world. Our communal feeling arouses intense fear and hatred when our community is threatened. We are ready to join in the common resistance, typically viewing the threatening other as subhuman. The moral sensitivities toward others within the community are muted in relation to those who threaten it. When the community is geographical, this leads to war. When the community is racial, it leads to oppression and exploitation. When the community is religious, it leads to persecution.

I believe that God calls us toward the recognition of the humanity of the threatening other and toward treatment that is appropriate to that recognition. I believe that many people have some recognition of the call. I also believe that the separation of "we" and "they" is a very powerful force inherited from the distant past and reinforced in many ways in contemporary society. This separation is so strong that most people act in terms of that force rather than in terms of God's call. Their decision to sin is celebrated by society as a moral act, so that for many people, God's call becomes faint indeed.

Deep-seated habits of obedience to authority are also a source of great evil. Wars would not be possible apart from this habit and its accentuation through military training and discipline. But is the habit as such evil? Surely, without the habit, human beings would not have survived and evolved. Children must act as their parents and teachers direct them even when they cannot understand the reasons for the action. This habit of obedience also enables those in authority to lead people in terrible directions. When the Germans obeyed their Nazi masters in genocidal acts against the Jews, were they sinning? Yes, I think that in particular instances, some knew that they were called to resist even at great personal cost. Few of us are in position to condemn those who failed to follow that call. Resisting authority when everyone else is obeying it is extreme heroism of a very rare sort. Probably God actually calls few to such actions.

What about Hitler? In his case can we regard personal sin as playing the primary role? I do indeed believe that God frequently called Hitler away from the course that he in fact followed. But I doubt that Hitler's refusal to heed that call is best understood in terms of simple perversity. I suspect that he really believed many of the things that he wrote and said. I suspect that he really believed that the reich he proposed to build was a thing of true worth and grandeur and that the sacrifice of much to this goal was morally acceptable. Even in his case, I suspect that erroneous beliefs played a larger role than sin.

Any analyses of this sort are extremely simplistic in comparison with the complexities of history and personal life. But I hope they explain why I do not feel the need to posit devils or demonize those individuals who seem to be particularly involved in causing evil. The ways in which even what is good in human nature and society can and does become destructive are so numerous and so effective that the mystery is how good sometimes triumphs over it. This is where I see the need to emphasize God's directing and empowering call to novel forms of goodness.

What is God's reason for allowing suffering? What is its nature?

The problem of theodicy is so basic that we need to approach it again and again from different points of view. It may be the theological issue that confronts believers with the greatest personal urgency. If a believer has any sense that God is responsible for what happens in the world and then encounters suffering in a vivid way, the question is inescapable: Why does God allow this?

Process thought softens the question by emphasizing that God does not control what happens. God always confronts a real world that is not of God's choosing. God works for the best outcome possible, but none of the possible outcomes may be good. All of them may include a great deal of suffering, and this suffering may be most severe with those who deserve it least.

This seems to be true of the whole world today. At this point we know of no way to prevent a great deal of suffering due to global warming. If humanity had responded quickly when scientists first identified this danger, extremely serious problems might have been avoided—but we did not. Although the many arguments put up against action have largely collapsed, our response is still drastically inadequate to do more than slightly slow the pressures we put on our environment. The global system seems to be such that feedback loops will accelerate the process of climate change.

Everyone will suffer, but the suffering will be unevenly distributed. The poor who are least mobile will suffer most as a rising sea level inundates populous deltas. They will be the ones least able to protect themselves from the spread of diseases. As prices for food and other necessities rise, it will of course be the poor who do without. The rich who have caused the global warming will be able to avoid, or at least postpone, the worst consequences.

How can we relate this terrible prospect to any kind of belief in God? If God cannot prevent drastically unjust suffering of this kind, of what use is God? To respond, let us put the question more positively in terms of what we, as process theologians, understand God to have been doing and is now doing.

In general terms, God is calling creatures to realize what value is possible in whatever situation they find themselves. This calling over billions of years transformed the surface of Earth from barren rock to a rich biosphere productive of innumerable forms of life. This, of course, did not reduce suffering. On the contrary, there was no suffering before the advent of life, but with every advance in sensitivity, suffering increased. The evidence before us is that God aims at the increase of value even when that involves also the increase of suffering. This suffering can be very horrible. Some scientists, such as Darwin, lost their belief in God as they reflected about the suffering that parasites sometimes inflict on their hosts.

This divine calling finally brought human beings into existence. Our appearance on the scene increased the total value in the world. Most process theologians think the increase was very considerable. It also increased enormously the amount of suffering, partly through the suffering inflicted by humans on other creatures. For example, the way we raise animals for meat causes more suffering in domestic animals than other animals ever inflicted on each other. The additional suffering goes far beyond that. Humans have exploited, enslaved, maimed, tortured, and slaughtered other humans on a scale incomparably greater than ever could have occurred among those creatures humans choose to call "beasts." Also, humans are, we believe, capable of greater depths of suffering than any other creatures. Finally, humans can and have destroyed their habitat along with that of other creatures to an extent previously inconceivable. Global warming is but one example.

Despite all of this, the evidence is that God supports the rise of conscious reflection and complex emotions that humanity brought into the biosphere. But that does not mean God simply observes it from a distance. God has always worked to direct the activities of this new species, through each of its members, away from mutual destruction and toward the broadening of horizons.

The pressure on individuals to conform to norms derived from the survival needs of the communities in which they exist is very great. God also supports the aim at survival, but God has called human beings to think of others, even those outside their own communities, even others not yet born. God has had some success. Hundreds of millions now subscribe to teachings of those who have invited them to live out of this wider vision.

These official beliefs do have some influence on the lives of many. Sometimes this wider vision breaks through to substantial historical influence as in Mahatma Gandhi, Martin Luther King, Jr., and Nelson Mandela. As Jesus noted, the established authorities, the rich, and the powerful find it particularly difficult to listen to this call when, as is usual, it threatens the status quo. Children and prostitutes are more likely to listen.

The interaction between human resistance to God's call and the physical reality of the world, which those profiting from present practices choose to ignore, generates a situation in which suffering is inevitable. That does not mean that God ceases to call us. Suffering is inevitable, but it may yet be reduced. If we do not heed the call, our responses to the inevitable suffering may only magnify it further. For example, in quarreling over what is yet available to us to meet our material desires, we may engage in nuclear war, the results of which could end our human story. At the other extreme, the crisis in which we are all plunged could bring us together as human beings for the first time, to work together to deal as humanely as possible with those who suffer. I have no doubt as to the future toward which God is now calling us. How much chance there is that we will listen and follow is another question.

What formal statements can we make now about God and human suffering? God does bear responsibility for human suffering in the sense that apart from God there would be no humans or any other beings capable of suffering. If we share with God the view that the increase of value, despite the accompanying increase of suffering, is a worthy goal, then we can love and worship the God whose creative work has brought us into being.

Human beings have a far wider range of choices than do the other creatures with whom we share the planet. Hence, with us God's call takes on a moral character. God calls us to broaden our horizons so as to include in our consideration the consequences of our actions for a wider and wider future. This makes it possible for us to "love our enemies." Sadly, it does not ensure that most of us will actually do so. We have for millennia experienced the horrors of not doing so. We have had a few magnificent indications of what is possible when we do so. It is not impossible that we will become more responsive to God. We can hope for a world in which suffering, and especially unjust suffering, will be much less prevalent.

Process theology emphasizes another side of the relation of God to suffering. For many centuries, despite biblical teaching, official Christian theology taught that God is immutable and, therefore, cannot be affected by our suffering. It was affirmed that even Jesus' suffering on the cross could not affect God and, therefore, that Jesus' divine nature did not suffer. Process theologians have been in the lead in rejecting this part of traditional teaching. More and more Christians realize that this idea of divine impassibility was imposed on the Bible from a philosophical teaching that we no longer see any reason to accept. Process thought is distinctive among these theologies, chiefly in that it provides a philosophical explanation and grounding for the view that God suffers with us in our suffering–and also rejoices with us in our joys.

This results from Whitehead's doctrine of prehension. A prehension is the way that the feelings of one occasion participate in constituting its successors. The best example to consider is the way your emotion in one moment is carried into the next moment. Whitehead said that one occasion of your experience prehends the preceding occasion. The previous experience flows into the new one. We can also describe this in terms of empathy. One experience has empathy for the preceding ones. It also feels the feeling in various parts of the body empathetically. One feels the ache in a tooth achingly. This empathy for our own immediate past and the experiences in our own bodies can also extend to those we love and, to some extent, imaginatively, even to those we do not personally know. In God, who is everywhere, empathy with creatures is universal.

So what about the charge that if God cannot prevent suffering, God is of no use?

Process theologians strongly disagree. It would be like saying that if parents cannot save their offspring from all suffering, they are of no "use." I employ this analogy because it is the one that comes most naturally to Christians. Our parents have given us life, with all its joys and sorrows. Ideal parents are always guiding and encouraging their children toward the good. They are there for their children whether the children in fact seek the good or not, and certainly when they fail to attain it as much as when they succeed. Their children's suffering causes them suffering. The parents rejoice with their children in their joys. True, they do not prevent them from suffering, often unjustly. But that does not mean that they are of no "use."

Obviously, human parents fall far short of these ideals even when they participate in them to some extent. In their case, self-interest is often in tension with concern for the children. While they really care for their children, they may also exploit them to boost their own egos. In God these limitations do not apply. This is not, from the process perspective, just a projection of our wishes onto the heavens. On the contrary, the nature of God is such that the tension between self-love and other love cannot exist. It is in and through creatures that God achieves the divine realization of value. Our good is God's good. Also the factors that make all human empathy imperfect are not found in God.

Of course, the word "use" cheapens the whole discussion. We do not praise and worship God because God is useful to us. We worship because God is worshipful, and we try to serve God out of the love and gratitude that God evokes. We seek to hear God's call because we know that call is to what is truly and ultimately the good. We know that apart from God our situation is truly hopeless. God is our hope for a better world. We know that whatever happens, all that we have been and now are will still matter because it matters to God. God saves us from meaninglessness.

God does not prevent suffering, but even suffering can be endured more easily when we know that we are not alone. Much suffering is not redemptive and cannot be redemptive either of us or of others. Some suffering can have positive results. God works in and through it to deepen our sensitivity to others, to hone our awareness of God, and to teach us to appreciate life and human companionship more fully. Indeed, the suffering involved in empathy with the suffering of others contributes to the richness and depth of our experience overall as well as giving a positive direction to our work.

Process theologians do not use arguments of this sort to imply that all that looks evil to us is, in fact, good in the whole picture. Much that looks evil to us is truly evil, countering God's purposes in the world. Because of God, much even that is truly evil can also be transformed in a way that wrings from it some good. As we face the onslaught of so much that is truly evil, we must do all we can to find ways to wring from evil such good as it allows. God makes that possible.

8

Christian Beliefs

Do you agree with David Griffin that appraisal of the evidence in the process perspective leads to belief in life after death? If so, should we anticipate rewards and punishments?

I will treat the question as twofold. First, if process thought allows (certainly without requiring) belief in personal continuity after death, What notions of rewards and punishments might be compatible with it? Second, What do I personally think about this?

The question is based on David Griffin's extensive discussion of the possibility of life after death and his investigation of the evidence in its favor. I am indebted to David for his extensive work. However, Griffin does not speculate much about what such life may be like, especially in relation to rewards and punishments.

With regard to what is consistent with what process thought affirms about God, it is best to begin with the metaphysically universal. The assumption must be that God relates to occasions occurring after physical death in much the same way that God relates to occasions occurring in this life. That means that God offers to them those possibilities that the total situation allows and encourages the best response. Ordinary ideas of divine punishment do not make any more sense for an afterlife than for this one.

We could imagine, however, that some of the causes of extreme injustice that operate in this life would not operate there. Presumably, distinctions of wealth and poverty do not apply. Nor can persons injure others by violent action. Presumably, there are no diseases. This would mean that one's condition would be more fully affected by one's own decisions. The inherently negative consequences of bad choices would be a form of punishment.

On the other hand, we cannot press this too hard. One's happiness is also deeply affected by the happiness or misery of those whom one loves. One's choices could influence but not determine the decisions of others that more directly shape their condition. Those whom one loves may continue to make themselves miserable. Perhaps, even more than here and now, it would be obvious that our lives are bound up with one another. We cannot be fully saved as individuals apart from the salvation of the whole community. Paul's eschatological vision in Romans 8 was, rightly, that of the liberation of the whole creation through the revelation of God's glory in and through the faithful. Nothing less would be true salvation.

Accordingly, the following question arises: Does this situation allow for real justice? That would require the suffering of those who have inflicted so much suffering on others. I think process thought has room for that, although not in the form of imposed punishment.

Let me emphasize the difference between imposed and inherent suffering. An addict may be punished by being imprisoned for crimes involved with the addiction. That is an imposed punishment. On the other hand, the addiction intensifies the suffering that may have led to it in the first place. This is inherent punishment. Furthermore, even if friends help the addict to break her or his addiction, this will not occur without a withdrawal, which includes a great deal of suffering. This, too, is inherent. God, I believe, calls many addicts to go through the suffering of withdrawal. Unlike the suffering of the addiction itself, this suffering is part of the path of salvation.

Something like that applies to all of us in varying degrees. Whether here or in another dimension, God calls us to purity of heart–to love God and creatures deeply. The highest happiness comes only to those who respond to this call. But the process of responding is painful. It includes some pain for all of us as we realize how we have hurt others whom we are now coming genuinely to love. These include others whom we have loved impurely. We have all experienced this in this life, as we have realized the unnecessary pain we have inflicted on parents, spouses, children, and close friends. As our love expands, we realize the pain we have inflicted on less intimate acquaintances and on persons we have not known at all. We realize that our style of life has profited from and reinforced economic systems that have been terribly harmful to the poor and to the Earth.

Some of us grow in this love and understanding during this life. We experience grief and repentance again and again. Our reward, even here, is the joy of a purer love. Continuing such growth after death would mean more pain, but the joy of growing love that accompanies that pain will more than compensate for continued suffering. Others of us may die without having ever examined ourselves from the point of view of other people or seriously considered the effects of our lives on them. Or we may have divided the world into "us" and "them" and been indifferent to the suffering of "them." For these people, the only path to joy lies through immense suffering. We can imagine God calling them into that suffering. We can imagine their resistance. Yet as long as the hardness of their hearts continues, it entails misery that will grow worse as time passes.

This is a vision of purgatory. Indeed, if some resist forever, it is a vision of hell. Since God does not coerce, this everlasting suffering might indeed be the destiny of some. It would postpone forever the full salvation of creation, but it would be a self-chosen destiny. The door to a suffering of purification or purgation would always be open. God would always be calling, persuading, and challenging the sinner to enter it.

C. S. Lewis vividly presented this kind of thinking about rewards and punishments after death in a book entitled *The Great Divorce.* The image there is of a hell in which the inhabitants make each other miserable by constantly putting each other down. Every day a bus appears to take them to heaven. Sometimes they get on, but when they arrive in heaven their behavior does not fit. They are even more uncomfortable there than in hell, so they return to hell.

The point, of course, is that the punishment for lovelessness is inherent in lovelessness. It is not imposed on people by God. God calls all people to love and never ceases to offer the opportunity to move in that direction. Loving others and receiving the love of others is blessed.

Another image emphasizes the theistic dimension more directly. Suppose we understand what happens at death as the beatific vision—that is, God, whom we experience so vaguely and uncertainly in this life, is present to all immediately and without ambiguity. For some, this is marvelous blessedness, just what they have longed for in this life.

For others, this is misery. In this life they have been able to ignore or domesticate God, or they have identified as "God" something that did not challenge them to change. They could occupy themselves with possessions and sensual delights and the acquisition of power or simply lose themselves in all sorts of distractions and entertainment. They have caused suffering in others and thereby in God as well and have experienced little true happiness themselves. They have not cared one way or another. Their whole structure of meaning has been based on assuming the unreality or irrelevance of the God who calls them to love others, including the "enemy," which has meant also the irrelevance of what happens to most other creatures. Suddenly, everything they have been appears false and evil. They have no defense, and they cannot lose themselves in something else. What is the beatific vision for some is hell for others.

Let me hasten to say that in depicting those who have wounded and denied God, I do not have in mind those honest seekers of truth who have, sometimes reluctantly and painfully, come to the conclusion that there is no God. If they long for truth and have lived in the quest for truth, the revelation of God who is the Truth would not be terrible for them. Quite the contrary! In most cases they would be confirmed in their denial of the reality of what the word "God" had meant to them. They would find joy in discovering that the whole of reality has still greater depths and meaning than their human quest had discovered.

The question asks for speculation, and I have gladly offered that. What would be most surprising would be to discover that my speculation, or anyone else's, corresponded closely to the reality.

Process thought is unapologetically speculative through and through. It seeks to find and tell the most likely tale. If the process thinker forgets the extreme limitations of the human mind in relation to the marvel of what is, valid and valuable speculation can turn into arrogant and destructive dogmatism. I do not know what happens at death, and I am suspicious of all who think they do. But for me, as one deeply shaped by the Christ event, the most likely tale is one about a God who loves all creatures and calls us to love one another. My speculations about life and death and whatever may lie beyond death are grounded in that.

Must salvation be attained prior to death as my fundamentalist friends insist?

The idea that our everlasting fate is settled at the moment of death has been widely held in Christendom, and not just by fundamentalists. Catholics softened it with their doctrine of purgatory. One might go straight to hell forever, but the majority of believers would not be ready for heaven. They would require purgation before they could enter their ultimately blessed destiny. The Reformers opposed the idea that anyone had personal merit and emphasized that salvation was a pure gift of God. They did away with purgatory. If you have faith, you go straight to heaven; otherwise, you go straight to hell. A variation on this involves soul sleep until the final judgment, when this "either-or" is applied. Your fundamentalist friends are continuing these traditions.

This view and its variation have a biblical basis. The parable of Lazarus and the rich man (Lk. 16:19–31) implies that once one is in hell, it is too late to repent. This parable of the final judgment indicates that at the end of history, people will be divided into the two groups. In Romans 2, Paul speaks of a final judgment that seems to be of a similar sort. This reflects the Pharisaic theology underlying much of early Christian thought.

On the other hand, many teachings in the New Testament do not fit this pattern. Jesus' central message, in continuity with the Hebrew prophets, was about the coming of the *basileia theou* (I like to translate this as "commonwealth of God") on Earth. Some will enter before others, but whether any are permanently excluded is not clear. Paul's eschatological vision in Romans 8 identifies the believers as the firstfruits of God's saving work, but the whole universe is to be liberated and glorified.

The question of what we can hope for has no single consistent answer in the Bible, or even in the New Testament. Christians are free to speculate about such matters based on clearer, more central teachings. One tradition of such speculation begins with the New Testament affirmation that God is love. Process thought generally operates within this tradition.

Those who take their cue from Jesus' revelation of God as love deny that people are punished in the crude sense. By this I mean that a loving God does not impose on people a useless suffering that is not the consequence of their own decisions and actions. If we refuse to believe that we are accepted and forgiven, we will suffer from our sense of guilt. If we refuse the love that others, including God, extend to us, we will suffer loneliness and alienation. God does not prevent such suffering. Also, we may judge that there are forms of suffering from which we learn or through which we grow. Love does not prevent a parent from inflicting that kind of suffering. The everlasting suffering in hell, which has no meaning other than sheer punishment, is not compatible with what we know of God as love.

Given this widespread agreement among process thinkers and many other Christians as well, the question remains whether one has opportunities after death to change one's spiritual condition. Some process thinkers believe that after death we live on in the life of God, but what lives on is what we have been up until that time. Such continuing life is certainly not punishment. God incorporates us into the divine life in the way that makes the most of what we have contributed. In agreement with your conservative friends, these process thinkers would say that we as agents no longer can change anything.

Other process thinkers believe that after death we experience a continuing personal existence in which new things happen to us and we engage in fresh actions. From a process perspective, as long as that continues to be the case, God will work lovingly with us for our good. These process thinkers agree with the idea that physical death does not end the possibility of repentance and new life.

A poem by Gerard Manley Hopkins depicts God as "the Hound of Heaven," pursuing those who reject God's gifts through all the ages, seeking to break down human resistance to divine blessing. I find this a beautiful image fully consistent with the revelation of God in Jesus.

Obviously, these images are not to be taken literally. The truth is that our attempts to think more literally about life after death do not get us very far. Your fundamentalist friends are right to put the emphasis on this life and the decisions that we make now.

Where process thinkers may differ from fundamentalists is that we do not focus attention on preparing for another life. We seek to love and serve God and God's creatures here and now, not in order to assure ourselves of a blessed life beyond the grave but because that is what we are now called to do. A life lived in that way is an appropriate response to God's grace whether or not it is continued beyond the grave. It is also the form of life in which we are most fulfilled here and now. It does not require an extension beyond death to be worthwhile.

Also, we do not expect so drastic a break between what we are in this world and whatever we may be beyond it. We may, however, experience a kind of intensification of our spiritual situation. Another image may bring that out. In this life we are always in the presence of God, completely known by God. However, it is relatively easy to ignore that fact and to live as though God were not. We may suppose that at death the veil is removed and the distractions are no longer available. We then find ourselves face-to-face with God.

Tradition has called this the beatific vision. For those who love God, this will be a moment of great fulfillment and blessedness. But even for most of them, the full awareness that they are wholly known may not be pure joy! Nevertheless, because the one who knows is the one who understands and forgives, the pain of fuller realization of his or her sin will be accompanied by the assurance of acceptance.

Others want to hide from the light but will find no place to hide. They must face the fact that they are fully known. They do not realize that the one who knows them is pure Love. They feel judged and condemned.

Such an image gives some support to the traditional Protestant emphasis that our condition at the last moment of life is important. This support in no way demands that no further change can occur. The new situation may produce repentance. Those who have failed to grow spiritually in this life may grow later on.

Of course, the sharp alternatives in this example are misleading. Most of us will find such an encounter with God both joyful and painful. We both long for God and fear closeness. We both want to be known and also to conceal. We are both justified and sinners, both saved and damned.

Perhaps the point of greatest difference between process theologians and your fundamentalist friends lies in the understanding of the spiritual state that is of greatest importance. The tendency of fundamentalists is to stress correct beliefs. We must believe in the Lord Jesus Christ as our savior.

Christian process theologians share the conviction of the great importance of Jesus Christ, but we react against any tendency to identify a particular formula of statements and beliefs as crucial to our salvation. A few years ago I coauthored a commentary on Romans with a New Testament scholar, David Lull. Many of the verses that have been taken to support the crucial importance of belief in Jesus Christ as savior come from Paul. What I learned from Lull is that the Greek word *pistis*, which has been translated as "faith," is usually better translated as "faithfulness." Paul is deeply moved by Jesus' faithfulness even to death for the sake of sinners. Paul calls us to participate in that faithfulness. Of course, this involves beliefs about Jesus and his crucifixion, but the question is not what we think with our minds but what we become in our total beings. To postpone becoming that to the moment of death means not to become that at all.

This shift from beliefs to the qualities of a faithful life also changes the way we can think about those who are not believers in Jesus. Surely the quality of life of some Jews is more faithful, when faithfulness is viewed against the background of Jesus' life and death, than some who hold orthodox Christian beliefs. It is not those who say "Lord, Lord" (Mt. 21:7) but those who are faithful who are saved. Christians should approach with great humility those who, sometimes for good reasons, have rejected the beliefs that Christians tell them they should accept. We believe they have been cut off from spiritual resources of great importance. Often we have cut ourselves off as well, especially by the judgmental spirit so strongly condemned by both Jesus and Paul. Viewed dispassionately, many who do not call themselves Christian have greater spiritual maturity than many who do. A loving God will not punish them for their failure to "accept" Jesus Christ as their Lord and Savior.

What kind of assurance can process theology offer?

It is painful to read that persons such as Mother Teresa did not have the inward joy and peace that they sought in their relation to God. She is certainly not alone. As a Methodist, it disturbs me that John Wesley sometimes asserted he was not a Christian because his inner state did not correspond with what he himself taught that an authentic believer should experience. Teilhard de Chardin, I think, also struggled with depression. Christian mystics have written of the dark night of the soul. One of the most moving novels I have ever read is Bernanos' *Diary of a Country Priest*.

I do not want initially to approach this question in terms of process metaphysics. We need to consider the phenomenon in itself. It seems to make clear that being a very sincere and active Christian, working effectively in the world, does not guarantee that one will be inwardly satisfied. Authentic virtue does not assure us of authentic happiness. Kant made quite a point of this lack of correspondence.

One response might be to suggest that people of this sort are driven by a hunger or a need of a psychological nature that cannot be satisfied by the method of extraordinarily virtuous activity they have chosen. I suspect that there is some truth to this, but I will not pursue it here. Disparaging psychological analyses of Wesley have much to feed on, but they do not end up explaining what is most important in his life work. No doubt we will be treated to similar analyses of Mother Teresa. Some people like these accounts because they cut truly extraordinary people down to our size, or even smaller.

A second response might be that the experiences of God that are sought are simply not a reality, that those who claim them are deluded. Hence, people of this sort are striving for what cannot be attained and they are too honest to share in comforting delusions. This is a view held not only by atheists and those who think of God in too impersonal a way to allow for the kind of relationship for which Wesley and Mother Teresa hungered but also by a good many mainstream Protestants.

For example, in the Lutheran tradition a common view is that confident acceptance of God's forgiveness is the source of assurance. Assurance is, of course, experiential, but it is an experience brought into being by faith, not by a personal experience of God. One believes that this faith is the gift of God. Again, faith is not an experience of God as such. This teaching does not necessarily depend on supposing that there are no immediate or extraordinary experiences of God. It does assume their occurrence is not to be expected or sought after.

How we place ourselves in regard to the reality and importance of "theistic experiences" is likely to depend on our personal life histories. I have had just one vivid experience of God's loving presence. In this case, it came unsought, and I do not anticipate any recurrence. Certainly, I have no idea as to anything I might do to bring it back. Because I treasure it, I cannot disparage interest in theistic experiences.

On the other hand, if I kept measuring my normal state of being or feeling against those few minutes of ecstatic experience, I would be depressed. That is, if I supposed that as a Christian believer I should continuously have a vivid sense of God's loving presence, I would certainly question the authenticity of my faith and become depressed. I think that Wesley's distressing comments about himself arose partly out of this sort of false expectation. Such expectation can also lead to self-deception. I can remember one period, at about age seventeen, in which I felt so strongly that as a faithful Christian I should be joyful that I tried hard to be so and acted more joyful than I really felt. I suspect that expectations of a type of experience that is quite rare and completely uncontrollable led to unnecessary disappointment in both Wesley and Mother Teresa.

Now we will turn to comments about this situation that are grounded in Whitehead's metaphysics. First, according to Whitehead, we experience (prehend) God all the time. Second, according to Whitehead, consciousness depends on the affirmation-negation contrast. We are conscious of what is sometimes present to us and sometimes absent. Since God is never absent, consciousness of God's presence is not to be expected.

For metaphysics these universal and inescapable, and therefore normally unconscious, aspects of experience are of special importance. Whitehead proposed that we can approach consciousness of them by imagining their absence. Consider one example of this method. Bertrand Russell proposed that nothing in any present experience gives evidence that there has been a past. This argument assumes the idea, widely accepted among philosophers, that all experience originates in sense experience. In Whiteheadian terms, presentational immediacy (sense experience) by itself does not relate us to a past.

We can perform the experiment of trying to experience the given world while not feeling any connection to the past. We find that we can do so only by removing some part of that experience—that is, the sense of the derivation of our present experience from past experiences. Since that sense is part of all experience whatsoever, it is normally not conscious, but when we try to imagine experience lacking any connection to the past, we can bring it to the fringes of consciousness.

We can do something of the same sort with the experience of God. Many nontheistic philosophers, who do not doubt that there is a relation to the past, suppose that everything that happens in the present must derive from that past. This leads them to some kind of determinism. We can try to imagine the experience of being totally constituted by the causal efficacy of the past. When we do, we again recognize that something is omitted, that our actual experience is one of choosing between alternative possibilities, however limited and however unpalatable all of them may be in some instances. We can dimly discern a relationship to possibilities as well as to the past actualities. For Whiteheadians, this is part of the universal experience of God.

Whitehead's most explicit discussion is found in *Religion in the Making,* where he went beyond the sheer presence of alternatives to talk about a rightness in things partly realized and partly missed. Once again we may try to imagine what our experience would be like if it contained no sense of better and worse. The effort to do so may lead us to recognize that there is some grading of value among the possibilities we confront. For Whiteheadians, this is also part of the universal experience of God.

This brings us to part of the question. Whitehead thought that we approach the potential rightness more or less closely. He did not discuss the psychological or spiritual consequences of doing so or of missing the mark more drastically, but it is not difficult to fill this in quite plausibly. Most of what we mean psychologically by "guilt" and "shame" seems to have more to do with social relationships than with the relationship to God. But we can discern the effects of the latter as well.

When one has acted in a way that misses the mark by a wide margin and is viewed as wrong or disgusting by the community whose views matter to one, that person may be troubled chiefly by the fear of being found out. As the danger of being found out fades, that person ceases to have much feeling about it. On the other hand, if one is found out, one will feel great shame or guilt.

Imagine a different situation in which one acts in a way that is viewed as wrong or disgusting by one's community but in which one believes was the best action that could be taken at the time. Some of the psychological feelings will still be the same. One may try to conceal what one has done and be distressed when one is found out. The conviction that whatever others may think and say, one did what was best in the circumstances changes the situation considerably. A person will not internalize society's condemnation but will find an inner assurance, even though one understands the barrage of condemnation and continues to find this emotionally very difficult to deal with.

The sense of being with the rightness in things plays a role even without a dramatic conflict with society. A person has a sense of wholeness that is not possible when one is aware of frequently missing the mark. The latter condition indicates that one's life includes elements that are in tension with the rightness in things, which nevertheless continues to make itself known.

Another consequence of largely conforming to the rightness in things is that this rightness expresses itself in increasingly refined ways. One becomes more sensitive to the feelings and needs of others and responds more spontaneously and appropriately. The rightness in things is never static or constant. What becomes possible as one attains it frequently goes beyond what was possible before, whereas missing the mark keeps lowering the mark for the future. All of this is experience of God.

This experience of God occurs whether one understands it as such or not. Often belief in God is an obstacle to this experience, because belief in God is so often bound up with legalism. Too often, believers suppress the sense of the rightness in things by identifying God's will for them with laws supposedly given by God. When atheism is the claim of freedom from such laws, an atheist may be more open to the rightness in things than the theist.

However, our theistic traditions all have a place for hearing God's call outside of legalistic teaching. Such hearing can overcome and replace the law. Then, theism can accent the importance of attuning ourselves to the ever-changing rightness in things and increase the sensitivity to that rightness, moment by moment. Whitehead's account should help us to strengthen this dimension of theistic teaching and living. My answer to the question is that living in harmony with the rightness in things does contribute to an experience of something that may well be called "assurance." This in no way means that one will be free from various sorts of psychological problems.

All the above refers primarily to experience of the primordial nature of God, although in light of the concluding paragraphs of Whitehead's *Process and Reality,* it may well involve the consequent nature as well. In any case, it is God as directing and calling that is involved. What about God's total empathy for us? Can that be experienced?

Whitehead's view that all of our experiences are taken up into the consequent nature of God is reassuring. Whitehead was convinced that this offered the assurance of fundamental meaningfulness or "importance" that we all need. Here, too, we can perform a hypothetical experiment of the sort proposed above. Can we believe that what happens totally disappears into nothingness? This would entail, for example, that there is no objective truth and falsity about the past. It is certainly possible to develop theories that have this consequence and even to act upon them. But I, for one, am doubtful that anyone really believes that. If I am right, then implicitly, people do believe in something like what Whitehead called "the consequent nature of God." Since most of them do not come to such a belief by a process of reasoning, there must be some, generally unconscious, experience of this side of God as well.

It is dangerous to introduce one's personal experience into a public discussion as I did earlier. Even if it has convincing power for the experiencer, it has no weight in argument for others. In this instance, even for me as experiencer, it did not prevent a subsequent period of thoroughgoing doubt.

I will only say that the experience I mentioned earlier, although it occurred long before I knew anything about process thought, felt like an experience of God in God's consequent nature. What was present felt fully actual, and the love that surrounded me was not that of calling me to act in the best possible way but simply accepting me as I was. It seemed to be a matter of prehending God's loving prehension of me. That was indeed wonderfully assuring.

If we assume that God is prehended unconsciously all the time by everyone, how is it that, from time to time, some aspect of God or of the relation to God becomes vividly conscious? I don't know. Perhaps the practice of some spiritual disciplines helps make this more likely, but that certainly had nothing to do with my case. We are free to practice disciplines of all sorts, but the only ones that are really attractive to me are those that heighten sensitivity to God's call. Disciplines that lead to altered states of consciousness no doubt have their value. They certainly produce interesting and impressive results. I believe it is better to expect less from all such efforts, rather than more. The same applies to virtuous action. Its effects on those to whom it is directed are sufficient reward, as is responsiveness to God's call in general. Whatever more may happen is pure gift, not to be anticipated in any way.

If God doesn't intervene, what is the point of intercessory prayer?

Insofar as we think of prayer as intending to have some effect on God, it is not just intercessory prayer, but all prayer that seems questionable to those who adopt the official philosophical theology of the church. We are told that God is immutable, that is, that nothing that happens can change God in any way. This theology is deeply influenced by typical Greek values. For most of the Greeks, invulnerability was greatly desired. One wanted not to be affected by what others thought and said and did, since one could not control that. Greeks sought to achieve invulnerability by seeking happiness in internal states that were not dependent on other people. They thought of God as perfect. For them perfection consisted in absolute invulnerability, or what they called impassibility. Nothing done by creatures could affect God.

For biblical writers, in contrast, perfection is perfect love. Jesus' love of human beings led him to protest the activities of the authorities and hence to being crucified. He was far from invulnerable. Early Christians thought that God is like Jesus, suffering with us in our suffering, rejoicing with us in our joy. God's perfection is perfect love. The lover is profoundly affected by what happens to the one who is loved. We process theologians believe they were right.

That means that this first reason for questioning prayer is invalid for us. We believe that everything we do and everything that happens to us affects God. God shares our joys as well as our sorrows. Although our experience changes and we soon forget the past, God is not like us. God's experience includes our experiences, not just while they are happening, but forever.

If everything we do affects God, then certainly prayer affects God. Because prayer is a special mode of experience, it affects God in special ways. Consider the prayer that God's will be done. Certainly the desired outcome is that we align ourselves with God. Such prayer is not simply an exercise in self-improvement. The openness to God inherent in prayer enables God's grace to work in us. God's grace actually leads us to be more in alignment with God's will.

I think many Christians understand this. We know that we cannot pray in Jesus' name for what is not in accord with God's purposes and desires. We also know that we cannot bring our own wills into alignment with God's purposes simply by an act of will. We turn to God for help, and we find that help in prayer.

Many Christians understand the value of prayer in this way, but they still find intercessory prayer mysterious. Yet much of our praying is for others, often for the health of someone who is ill. In many ways this seems the most Christian form of prayer. We believe that God wants health and works for health, so we can pray for the health of others in Jesus' name. But how does this help?

It is easy to see that by praying for another we may be expressing and deepening our concern. Perhaps we are more likely to pay a visit or send a card. But our sense is that the purpose of intercessory prayer is not only that we be changed but that an improvement occurs in another. How that can work is another question.

Much of the problem in understanding this comes from modern thought and its special expression in the sciences. Most Christian teaching in recent centuries has tried to adjust to this. This effort creates a serious tension, since modern thought is very different from biblical thought.

Standard modern thought is based on a model of reality derived from clocks. Clocks are based entirely on pushes and pulls between material bodies. The great medieval clocks that inspired this kind of thinking not only told time but also played music and put on little dramas with figures that came out each hour. The idea was that the whole of nature could be explained as complicated clockwork. The vast majority of scientific explanation still employs this model.

Many Christians have accepted this view of nature and then added that God can overrule natural occurrences and work miracles. If we think this way, then most of our intercessory prayers are asking God to interfere in the natural order and do something that conflicts with it. Many other Christians, even those who accept this view of nature, think that if such supernatural interventions occur at all, they are very rare. They are hesitant to pray for them. Some people really dislike the idea of God's breaking the laws of nature.

Of course, in the time when the Bible was written, nature was understood very differently. Biblical persons did not know of scientific laws that nature observed. God was very much involved with nature, and sometimes God's involvement led to astonishing consequences. These were called "miracles." Most, although not all, miracles were matters of abrupt healing, what today we would call "faith healings."

Those who effected such healings were highly revered and sought after, but they were not doing something "supernatural."

Process theologians are closer to the Bible than to modern thinking. We believe God works in every natural event. In general, we can say that God's working is for life and health in animate things. Human beings have many blockages to health. Some blockages are psychological and some are spiritual. God works to overcome these. The attitude and belief of the sick person plays a large role in the degree of God's success. The presence of one who inspires assurance can make a large difference. Hence, when Jesus tells people that their faith has healed them, this makes sense to us.

Of course, Jesus did not mean that people simply heal themselves by adopting the right attitude. The healing is ultimately enacted by God. Faith removes some of the obstacles to God's working. The faith is often in response to the healer, who in the gospels is usually Jesus.

Furthermore, it is equally important for us to note that psychological and spiritual factors are not the only ones that affect health. Their change does not automatically result in healing. Believing that we can set aside all other considerations leads to self-deception. We know that the "healings" of some faith healers today are sometimes quite partial or quite temporary. Exaggerated emphasis on the role of subjective attitudes in healing can lead to feelings of guilt when one's prayer does not result in healing. Blaming the sufferer for suffering only makes matters worse.

Now what about intercessory prayer? What I have already said indicates that the boundary between the physical and mental worlds is much more fluid than many people suppose. Our emotions and attitudes are greatly affected by the condition of our bodily organs, but the condition of those organs is also greatly affected by our emotions and attitudes. Now I add that we are far less separate from one another than we usually suppose. The emotions and attitudes of those around us have a great influence on our own.

Modern people who acknowledge all of this suppose that it all depends on awareness of the emotions of others based on sensory cues. Accordingly, for one to pray in church for the healing of someone who is in a hospital miles away still does not seem to make any sense. Yet we do this all the time. Does process thought change the situation?

Process theology holds to a different understanding of reality, one that is closer to that of people in biblical times. We believe that our experience of one another is not all mediated by sensory cues. We actually feel the feelings of others much as we feel the feelings of the cells in our own bodies. These relations are not limited to immediate proximity. Modern thinkers still resist the notion of action at a distance. In fact, the evidence for this in physics is now beyond dispute. We have long possessed evidence for this action at a distance even with regard to human experience. That intercessory prayer can have an effect on someone who is not present does not violate the known facts. The problem is that the common worldview of the modern world has not been adjusted to account for these facts. Process thought can readily accommodate them.

One further question remains: Is there a difference between intercessory prayer and simply holding people lovingly in our thoughts and envisioning them as healed? Probably not much. Still, I favor the form of prayer. Ultimately, it is God who heals. Because of God, the body works in complex ways for its own healing. Intercessory prayer should never be an effort to get God to do what God does not want. We should not be pleading with God to act in a way that God resists. It is, instead, to put our thoughts and feelings into the mix in such a way that God's purposes can be better realized. God empowers us, but we also empower God. Indeed, God empowers us to empower God. To hold up a loved one before God, making our thoughts and feelings available to God to help overcome obstacles to God's healing work in that person—that is authentic intercessory prayer. It is not magic, but it can make a difference.

A final word of caution. Sometimes Christians seem to feel that prayer is a particularly Christian activity. Jesus does not lift it up in this way. Jesus calls on us to give water to the thirsty. If a man asks for water that you could provide, and instead of giving it, you pray for him, this prayer is not an expression of Christian piety. If instead of visiting a sick woman in the hospital, you pray for her at home, nothing about that prayer is pious. To withhold needed medical care and substitute prayer is not a Christian act. We are called by Jesus primarily to serve our neighbors in whatever ways we can.

Intercessory prayer can be one form of service. It is not a substitute for more obviously effective forms. We properly pray for people to supplement other forms of service or when we have no other way to help them.

The primary reason for engaging in prayer, even intercessory prayer, is to bring our own purposes in line with those of God. If God uses that new alignment to benefit the one for whom we pray as well as ourselves, that is a wonderful bonus.

Many process theologians seem to shy away from the doctrine of the Trinity, but isn't a trinitarian understanding of God essential to Christian faith?

I am one of those process theologians who have shied away from the *doctrine* of the Trinity. I accent "doctrine" because I strongly believe that the biblical language that has given rise to the idea of the Trinity is important and that much of what the doctrine has represented in the past is to be affirmed. The doctrine is very obscure, however, and too often the church has employed it as a club against faithful believers. The doctrine of the Trinity has also led to the idea that we should believe what in fact makes no sense to us because the church tells us to. That has done great harm. Such thinking has nothing to do with what Paul called *pistis*, a Greek word we translate as faith or faithfulness.

I will have more to say about the harm done by trinitarian doctrine in the history of the church, but first I want to say what I think is centrally important in the ideas that have given rise to the doctrine. Most of the discussion in the early church that eventuated in this doctrine centered on the incarnation of God in Jesus. The issue was twofold. Was the Divine really constitutively present in Jesus? Was the divine that believers found in Jesus truly God?

The church answered both of these questions affirmatively. From a process point of view, the answers were confusing because they were built around the category of ousia, or substance. That is not our issue at the moment. Given the options, the answers were the right ones.

The answer to the second question is what led to the development of trinitarian thought. The Divine that was incarnate in Jesus was truly God. Yet the New Testament account depicts a filial relationship of Jesus to the one he called Abba, or Papa. In the most explicit texts on this topic, that which is incarnate in Jesus is identified as Logos (word) or Sophia (wisdom). Some passages suggest it was Pneuma (spirit). Any of these divine realities could be considered as creatures of God rather than truly God. That would mean that a preexistent reality other than God became flesh in Jesus. The church said no: that which became flesh in Jesus was truly God, not a demigod or a creature of God. This meant that within God one must distinguish what Jesus called Abba from what was incarnate in him. This entails a duality in God—Father and Son, with Logos identified with the Son.

Given the choices the church faced in the early centuries, I approve these moves. Nevertheless, they led to serious problems. It was important to the church to deny the existence of two gods. In the interest of defending the unity of God, the church insisted that although there might be rhetorical reasons for associating actions of God with one or another of the two, in fact both were involved in all God's acts—except one: Only the Son or Logos was incarnate in Jesus. This was required to project the filial relationship of the human Jesus to his heavenly Father into the Divine that was incarnate in him.

I do not believe the church had any real need for this projection. It was part of a pattern of failing to distinguish clearly between what was incarnate in Jesus and Jesus as the one in whom the Divine was incarnate. This confusion led to talk of Jesus as preexisting, even from eternity, and being identical with the Divine that was incarnate in him. Then the second Person of the Trinity becomes a divine human being instead of a purely divine being. Jesus becomes a member of the Trinity. I oppose trinitarian doctrines that move in this direction unless they emphatically abandon other aspects of traditional trinitarian teaching.

Part of the confusion here comes from the baptismal formula. I believe that the "Son" in whose name we are baptized is properly the human Jesus in whom God was incarnate. Christians were baptized in the name of the Father, who is God; the Son, who is Jesus; and the Holy Spirit. We will return to the Holy Spirit in rounding out the Trinity. The first Christian generations held no thought that these three had identical metaphysical status. The New Testament writers assumed that Jesus was a creature who was born, matured, died, and was raised by God. He was not an eternal being. "Son" became used to refer both to Jesus and to the eternal Logos. At that time it became "heretical" to point out the difference, and the consequences were disturbing.

In any case, the first step toward the doctrine of the Trinity was to make a distinction within God in order that what was said to be incarnate in Jesus was not God as a whole but one Person of

God, distinct from another Person, who was identified as "Father." To avoid polytheism, the church insisted that the distinct Persons shared the same substance. Once this distinction was allowed, that is, that more than one divine being could share a single substance, the church had no conceptual difficulty in similarly hypostatizing other terms by which the Divine had been named, such as Sophia and Pneuma. In fact, this was done with Pneuma and not with Sophia. Later it was almost done with Mary, although never officially. Probably the baptismal formula was the reason that we ended up with these three Persons.

That multiple Persons have a common substance can be understood in diverse ways. In the East, the tendency was to image the Persons as quite concrete and the substance they shared as more abstract. The substance was understood more as an essence, so that just as three men share the essence of male humanity, the three divine Persons share divinity. To avoid polytheism, the theologians emphasized how profoundly the three were constituted by their mutual relations.

In the West, the tendency was to emphasize the substantial unity and identity of the three "Persons." The threeness was viewed in terms of aspects of the one God. When Augustine reflected about this threeness, the New Testament distinctions almost disappeared. What seemed important was just to show how three can be one and one can have three discriminated aspects or features. The church assumed that a Christian must accept the trinitarian doctrine, even though any real theological reason for affirming this threeness had ceased to function in an important way.

We have, then, one trinitarian formula interpreted in two markedly different ways. The first tends to tritheism. The second tends to make distinctions for the sake of conforming to the formula rather than because there are issues of spiritual importance at stake.

Obviously, I have moved to criticism. I want to return to what is positive. The early church enjoyed vivid experiences of the Spirit. Paul is an important source for our understanding of this phenomenon. The Spirit was a felt and transforming divine presence. The theoretical question was whether this divine reality was truly God. The church agreed that it was. To me that is extremely important. God as God is present in the world and in the church, transforming individuals and communities. When this sense of divine presence fades, the church loses its vitality.

Some people who speak of the importance of the Trinity to Christians mean only that it is important to emphasize God the Father, Jesus as God's unique incarnation in history, and the Holy Spirit as God's presence in nature and in human life. I agree that this is central to Christian understanding. The right balance of these three is critical to healthy faith and Christian community. If this is what is meant by those who say that to be Christian is to be trinitarian, I am an ardent trinitarian and find this way of thinking eminently congenial to process thought.

Furthermore, in many ways the process understanding of God is more supportive of trinitarian thought than the classical view of the divine simplicity. This classical doctrine conflicted directly with the idea of trinitarian distinctions within God and added to the paradoxical character of the whole teaching.

In contrast, Whitehead unparadoxically distinguished two natures of God and, on one occasion, even referred to a third. A good Whiteheadian is, therefore, necessarily a trinitarian, but the three natures identified with Whitehead do not usefully correspond with biblical language about Father, Son, and Spirit.

More relevantly, Whitehead expressed great appreciation for the Alexandrian Fathers who worked at showing how the three persons were constituted by their internal relations with one another. He thought they made an extremely important metaphysical breakthrough, which his own philosophy generalized. The problem for a process theologian is not with the philosophical ideas but with their being limited to narrowly theological doctrines and to solving a problem that was originally generated in a somewhat artificial way.

The process objection is that the doctrine of one substance in three persons does not help us today to make the important Christian assertions the church needs. Both the standard Eastern and the standard Western formulations lead us astray. Insistence on the three-in-one doctrine, when it has no beneficial use in Christian life, is an authoritarianism that is alien to authentic faith.

In conclusion, let us consider a recently discovered strength of the Eastern doctrine. According to this teaching, God is a kind of community. This idea works against the extreme individualism of the Enlightenment and supports the idea that human beings should also constitute themselves as communities. These results are certainly attractive to process thinkers. However, the doctrine still seems somewhat ad hoc. It seems that we are stuck with a doctrine for which we have to find some use. It does not seem to reflect biblical thought, and it lends currency to the serious criticisms of Jews and Muslims.

This doctrine of divine community is used in support of *creatio ex nihilo* (creation out of nothing). For me, this is not in its favor. A theological argument for a process view of an everlasting creation is that the very being of God is relational. An increasingly common move against this position is to assert that before there were creatures to love, the three persons of the Godhead loved one another. This again accents the tendency toward a tritheistic understanding of the Trinity that is not congenial to process thought and seems to posit a form of love that is very different from that of which the Bible speaks and which is revealed in Jesus.

Many process theologians do not share my critique of the doctrine of the Trinity. Indeed, some prize this doctrine very much for reasons that I have noted, as well as for other reasons. I myself have tried to develop positive trinitarian formulations in the collection of essays in *Trinity and Process,* edited by two enthusiastic process trinitarians, Joseph Bracken and Marjorie Suchocki. Their own contributions to process trinitarianism are impressive. Process thought can make significant contributions to what is now a rather fluid discussion of trinitarian doctrine, thanks largely to Jürgen Moltmann. My critical comments, therefore, reflect personal concerns with the way the doctrine has traditionally functioned more than any general opposition to employing a process perspective with respect to it.

9

Religious Pluralism

What is the relationship between process, evangelical, and liberal theologies?

I appreciate this question. In the national meetings of the American Academy of Religion, the only sessions in which process theology as such now plays a large role are those of a group called Open and Relational Theologies. This was organized by Tom Oord, a Wesleyan evangelical committed to process theology, to continue the discussion between "open theologians" coming out of the evangelical community and process theologians coming chiefly out of the liberal community. These sessions have been well attended, with the majority of participants coming from the evangelical side. Few liberals, other than process folk, attend.

Now the questions are (1) why are a good many conservative evangelical theologians interested in conversation with process theologians and (2) why are so few liberals interested? I will deal with the first question briefly and the second at greater length.

First, conservative evangelicals in the academy are strongly interested in theology in general. Many of them, of course, are conservative in a way that leads them to reject process theology as a whole with little examination. However, others recognize the internal puzzles in the inherited theology and that some revisions are needed to avoid absurdities. An inner dynamism among these conservative evangelicals leads them to raise many of the questions that the liberal tradition in general, and process theologians in particular, have been dealing with for some time. Many of these evangelicals are willing to set aside their negative prejudices and entertain proposals for solving their theological problems even if these proposals come from the liberal tradition.

For most evangelicals, these proposals must be tested biblically more than philosophically. This does not mean a total rejection of philosophy. In any case process theologians have long claimed that many of our teachings are more biblical than those of classical theism. We are glad to engage conservative evangelicals on these grounds, even if our assumptions about biblical authority differ.

Among conservative evangelicals, the ones most likely to be interested in this conversation are the Wesleyans. Wesley was certainly an evangelical, but he rejected Calvinist views of God's total control on biblical grounds and for the sake of evangelism. Many conservative Wesleyans are restive under the dominance, and sometimes domination, of the conservative Calvinist evangelicals, who are sometimes strict fundamentalists. This movement among conservative evangelicals is today led by "open theologians," and the dialogue between them and process theologians is a promising and lively one.

The answer to the second question of why liberal theologians are not interested in dialogue with process theologians depends, obviously, on what we mean by liberals. If we are talking about the church, then the statement is quite wrong. Process theology gets a good hearing from open-minded laity and clergy today, a better hearing, I think, than at any time in the past. Conservative church people, in contrast, are rarely interested, even if some of their theologians are. From the point of view of the church, therefore, an entirely different projection would be needed.

The difference in the role of process theology in the academy and in the church is an indication of the great distance between these. In the academy, "liberal" theology has developed a narrower meaning. It has become a label that relatively few now apply to themselves.

Historically, liberal theology developed as an effort to continue the Christian tradition in an increasingly inhospitable intellectual and cultural context by adapting its teaching to that context. Liberals appropriated the results of the natural and social sciences and showed how Christian faith, rightly formulated, could be understood in a way that did not conflict with that new understanding. Liberals appropriated the results of historical study of Christian scriptures and church history and showed how these supported transformation of Christian teaching. Liberals opened themselves to the many criticisms of Christianity and sought to reformulate the faith in ways that did not continue the evils done in the past in the name of Christianity. Liberals recognized truth and goodness in other religious traditions and sought to formulate Christian beliefs in a way that did not reject these. Process theology is a form of liberal theology in all of these ways.

This openness has led much of the liberal movement to reject the theological task altogether. Theology is no longer appreciated in wide circles of liberalism, both in the church and in the academy. In the academy, this expresses itself in religious studies, which typically contrast themselves with theology in that they describe theological literature and practice from a neutral, uncommitted point of view. Such practitioners regard themselves as independent of any particular faith perspective. Many are, in fact, Christians, and some are active church members. They do not, however, think of their work as directly related to their faith or to any attempt to articulate normative statements about matters of religious concern. Process theology has every reason to learn from religious studies, but for the most part those active in religious studies show little interest in process theology. From the point of view of many of them, the commitment of process theology to the Bible, the tradition, and the church, as well as its normative philosophical interests, seems out of date.

Other former liberals have moved from liberal theology to liberation theology. They have become Latin American liberation theologians, feminist theologians, black theologians, and so forth. In the broad spectrum of theologies, many of them may still be considered "liberal," but for the most part they criticize liberalism. Associating liberalism with comfortable middle-class interests, they state their views in contrast to it. Insofar as they identify process theology with the liberal theology they criticize, little dialogue is possible. Fortunately, process theologians have been quite open to their criticisms and have incorporated much of the liberationist spirit. Gradually, liberation theologians are recognizing points of contact and possibilities of mutual support. Feminist theologians have a long history of positive relationships with process theology. The situation is improving on other fronts. But this does not mean that liberationists have become more "liberal."

Many former liberals joined the neoorthodox movement in the middle of the twentieth century. Neoorthodoxy is by no means as strong today as it was forty years ago, but its basic impulse persists–to affirm traditional Christian teaching in considerable independence of our knowledge of other fields. Today this impulse is dynamically represented in postliberal theology, in "radical" orthodoxy, and among some who make use of deconstructive postmodernism. Process theology stems from that segment of the liberal movement that did not move in that direction.

Nevertheless, process theology appropriated much of the criticism of earlier forms of liberalism, especially as articulated by Reinhold Niebuhr. This separated it from other forms of liberalism that did not do so. These other forms of liberalism have tended to take the viewpoint of the Enlightenment as normative and to limit Christian theology to what can be said in those terms. Process theology has participated in the critique of the Enlightenment and of those liberal theologians who continue to adjust Christian formulations to its principles.

This adjustment by what we may call "Enlightenment liberals" generally leads to attempts to solve the theological problem by affirming less and less. Too many recent liberals are much clearer about what they do not believe than about what they do believe. This is not where process theology wants to go. We have actually had rather little serious dialogue with those liberals who do move in this direction. Of course, we support them in many of their negations, but our focus is on providing a positive Christian alternative.

We share with Enlightenment liberals in rejecting a number of traditional doctrines. For example, we reject the doctrine of divine omnipotence. We do so for the sake of the gospel, which we believe presents us with a very different idea of divine power. We do not think that we believe less than do more traditional Christians, or in a less biblical or Christian way, when we emphasize that God's power is the power to liberate and empower us rather than to replace our power with God's. We do not think that we believe less because we believe that God's incarnation in Jesus makes Jesus more fully human rather than subtracting from his humanity. We do not think that we believe less when we insist that God is a living presence in our lives, creatively transforming us.

We believe that God's love is inclusive of all and that God seeks the salvation of all. We believe that this calls us to work for peace and justice everywhere. We believe that women share fully in humanity and relate to God just as men do. We believe that this means that both church and society should give women all the opportunities for self-expression and leadership that are available to men. We also believe that human beings belong to the created order, sharing this with other creatures. We believe that this calls us to give up our arrogant anthropocentrism and to seek the good of the whole of creation. We believe that all of this is the deeper teaching of the Bible, seriously obscured in the Western tradition. This, to us, is not a watering down of traditional teaching but a realistic and enlivening formulation of the gospel.

Another development in the latter part of the twentieth century has separated process theology from many liberals and also from many liberationists and postliberals. This development is the linguistic turn that has played so large a role in philosophy as well as theology. This is a turn away from questions of how the world actually is and, especially, of whether there is a divine reality of any kind. Such questions are replaced by a focus on language. It is held that language is the reality that constitutes our world. Language, thus understood, does not refer to anything beyond itself. One bit of language is to be explained in terms of other bits of language.

What difference does it make whether one speaks of God or of "God"? That is, what difference does it make whether one is interested in ontological or metaphysical reality or accepts the idea that language is the comprehensive world in which we live and move and have our being? In other words, what difference does it make whether language refers to something beyond itself or all references are internal to language?

For process theologians it makes a lot of difference. This difference is what makes interaction with ordinary church folk and with conservative evangelicals natural, while making communication with many in the academy difficult. Process theologians, most believers in all our churches, and conservative evangelicals agree that God is far greater than we can think, but also that some ideas about God are truer than others. For all of us, the question of whether God controls everything that happens is a real question and not one about how language is used. The question of whether we are really loved, regardless of how other human beings treat us, is a real question. Whether there is something more than human that works for good in the world is not a matter of language alone; our existential hope depends on what answer convinces us. Whether the natural world is imperiled by human greed and exploitation is a real question whose answer does not depend on our choice of language. For those who have taken the linguistic turn, these are not real questions, since there is nothing to talk about beyond the language that we use.

Of course, we can engage in dialogue with liberals who have taken the linguistic turn. But the dialogue cannot be about God and human beings and the natural world. It has to be, first, about whether language has a referential character. In my experience, those who operate with the assumption that it does not are rarely eager to discuss the issue. As long as they are committed to this assumption, the topics that process theologians most want to discuss cannot come to the table.

Much theology today is denominational. Theologians identify themselves as Lutheran, Reformed, Greek Orthodox, Roman Catholic, Pentecostal, and so forth. Among these theologians, some are more liberal and some are more conservative. Process theologians can talk more comfortably with the liberals in each tradition than with the conservatives. In each of these communities, some theologians make use of process thought. Still, there is no widespread eagerness of denominational theologians, even the more liberal ones, to enter discussions with process theologians.

Is this account a rebuke to liberal theology? Perhaps. It is also an expression of regret that liberal theology has largely faded from the academic scene. Process theology is in greater continuity with the liberal tradition than is any other lively current movement, but it also distances itself from much that is now generally understood as "liberal theology." We claim to be a form of postmodern or post-Enlightenment theology, although we also believe this is the proper form for the liberal tradition to adopt today. We want to break with the Enlightenment, not by abandoning its effort to understand reality but by proposing a major shift in the way to understand it. We think this shift can be a great gain for faith. We believe that avoiding the problems of the Enlightenment by abandoning the effort to understand a reality beyond language is a dead end intellectually and deeply destructive of religious faith.

Is our objection that liberal theology is too preoccupied with the understanding of human beings? Perhaps. Insofar as the focus on human beings is due to the radical dualism of either Descartes or Kant, we deplore it. Abandoning discussion of the world and of God is a retreat that we want to reverse, but we certainly do not disparage the study of human beings. I have already noted our great indebtedness to Reinhold Niebuhr. I should also mention the importance for us of the existentialists. We have had our eyes opened to much about human beings through the work of feminists. Obviously, I could go on and on. The problem is not too much study of human beings; it is the study of human beings and their history in isolation from the study of the natural world and of the divine.

Are there similarities between Eastern Orthodoxy and process theology?

I believe affinities exist between process theology and Eastern Orthodoxy. To speak of this in short compass, I will throw all scholarly scruples aside and make some sweeping generalizations about three great families of theologies: the heirs of the Reformation, the Roman Catholics, and the Eastern Orthodox. I will then locate process theology in relation to these.

The Reformers eschewed any systematic use of metaphysics. Not all Protestants have followed in this rejection, but it remains the mainstream view in the denominations most influenced by them. The rejection was strongly reemphasized in the twentieth century by Neo-Reformation theology. Thus Reformation theology has followed Luther and Calvin in their aim to be biblical, even when in its recent forms it fully recognizes the need to take critical biblical scholarship seriously and to reinterpret the Bible in multiple and changing contexts. Today the systematic rejection of metaphysics often entails the abandonment of realism, that is, of any claim that God exists in God's self, so that our beliefs about God are, objectively speaking, more or less accurate or true. In place of this, theologians in this tradition often emphasize that the language of Christian faith constitutes a self-contained whole within which, and within which alone, words like "God" have Christian meaning.

From the point of view of process theology, despite the Reformation's intention to eschew philosophical influence, the influence remains. Theologians who claim the heritage of the Reformation often interpret the Bible through the classical creeds and later theological developments. Their understanding of God and of incarnation is often informed by traditional ways of thinking that are heavily influenced by Greek thought. They sometimes read Anselmian views of the atonement back into biblical texts. The insistence that they are not philosophical often makes them more resistant to criticism of their philosophical assumptions. We think those who recognized that the rejection of metaphysics is also the rejection of philosophical realism are astute, but we consider their consequent abandonment of realism a move that in the long run proves disastrous for faith.

Roman Catholics in general have followed Augustine and Thomas in making systematic use of philosophical categories. Both Augustine and Thomas contributed to philosophical reflection from their Christian perspectives, so the philosophies they adopted were also adapted for Christian use. However, the notion of substance, quite absent in the Bible, has played an important role in this theology. Even when the notion of substance is not explicitly used, it shapes much of the thinking of Roman Catholic theologians. The perfection they usually attribute to God seems more informed by the ideals of the Greeks, especially of Aristotle, than by those of the Bible.

From the point of view of process theology, Catholic theology has been right to recognize that the questions discussed by philosophers are meaningful and, indeed, inescapable for the full articulation of faith. The Christianization of philosophy also seems to us entirely appropriate and necessary. For many centuries the best, almost the only, philosophies available were those of the Greeks. Plato and Aristotle offered the fullest and most brilliant philosophical positions. The church was wise to adopt and adapt their ideas. Nevertheless, to a greater extent than Roman Catholics have generally acknowledged, the philosophies they adopted embodied ideas and values that are in serious tension with those of the Bible. They are also in tension with developments during the modern period. In some instances we believe that the church has been wise to resist modernity, but not in all. We believe that a profound shift from substance categories to those of process would liberate Catholic thought from excessive bondage to Aristotle. It could then become both more biblical and in less tension with cutting-edge developments in the sciences.

Eastern Orthodoxy is also a philosophical theology. It, too, relied on the Greeks for philosophy. I should acknowledge the very limited knowledge I have of this tradition, but I shall proceed with offering my impressions. The East adopted Platonic forms of thought more than Aristotelian. It did not separate theology from philosophy as sharply. As a result, it produced a worldview that Christianized the philosophy it adopted more fully than did the West. Also it did not establish as tight a philosophical orthodoxy as that which developed in the West. Gregory of Nyssa remains the single most influential synthesizer, but his writings do not offer as fixed and finished an account of all things as did Thomas Aquinas. Hence the contemporary situation seems more fluid. The idea of substance is certainly present in this vision of reality, but it does not seem to control what is said in the same way as in Thomistic theology in the West.

Process theology shares with Eastern Orthodoxy the influence of Plato. It shares the blurring of lines between philosophy and theology. Precisely because Orthodox thought seems less rigidly fixed than Roman Catholic, process theology finds it possible to interpret many of the formulations of Orthodox theologians in ways that are highly congenial to Whitehead. We held a conference of process theologians and Orthodox theologians in Claremont some years ago that revealed large overlaps in our philosophical theologies. Of course, we had disagreements also, but overall our philosophical theology seemed closer to the Orthodox than to either the heirs of the Reformation or Roman Catholics. An interested reader could ask the Center for Process Studies for copies of some of the papers presented at that conference.

I was again impressed by the possibilities of coming together through working with a doctoral student from the indigenous Christian church of India. This church traces its source to the mission of St. Thomas, after whom it names itself. Historians may doubt the accuracy of this history, the records of which were destroyed by Portuguese Catholics, but that it is very ancient cannot be doubted. Its theological and liturgical connections have been with the Syrian Orthodox, although the branch that now calls itself "Mar Thoma" has been deeply influenced by an Anglican form of modern Protestant theology. This student, George Pothen, had been teaching theology at the Mar Thoma seminary and came to Claremont to study Whitehead and Gregory of Nyssa. One who wants to examine the congeniality of the philosophical theologies of these two thinkers, coming out of extremely different contexts, should read his dissertation.

This congeniality has had practical results. I was seriously involved in only one major conference of the World Council of Churches. This was focused on science, technology, and Christian faith and held at the Massachusetts Institute of Technology. Most of the work was done in sections with twenty to fifty members. Original plans called for only one theological section, assigned the topic of "faith and science." It was understood that faith and science are two ways of viewing the world, that is, it was assumed that theological discussions today would be about ways of knowing–epistemologies. This reflected the dominance of the Reformation tradition. However, two members of the organizing committee objected. One was Charles Birch, a process thinker. The other was Bishop Gregorius, an Indian from the other branch of the indigenous church, which calls itself Syrian Orthodox, and one who had himself written on Gregory and Whitehead. These two men insisted that theology not only is a matter of epistemology but also includes beliefs about what really is. They persuaded the committee to organize an additional section dealing with nature, humanity, and God. For those of us with metaphysical interests it seems important to talk about God and nature and not only about how human beings come to their beliefs on these topics.

I ended up chairing this section. Both Orthodox and Catholics participated, and I think our results were good. However, the outcome reflected how deeply we are all rooted in our histories and how different are the histories of East and West. However close process theology may come to some philosophical theologies of Eastern Orthodoxy, as a historical phenomenon it belongs to a different world. We process thinkers in the West are shaped by our Western history that includes the Renaissance, the Reformation, the Enlightenment, the long discussions about faith and science, the sexual revolution, and recent waves of liberation thinking. None of this has had much impact on Eastern Orthodox thinkers. We Westerners see our relation to the earliest Christian communities as a broken one. In the East the relation seems fully continuous. They read the New Testament in its original language. We read it in translation.

The consequence of these differences showed up in our work as a committee and especially in its aftermath. The committee felt the need for Christians to confess our collective sins and failures in relation to nature. We recognized that much of the traditional teaching of the Western churches had viewed nature dualistically and anthropocentrically, and we called for repentance. We knew that from the point of view of the Eastern Orthodox, the church cannot be sinful, and we also knew that in fact Eastern teaching had not been nearly as dualistic or anthropocentric as that in the West. This is a point of contact and an area in which process theologians and other contemporary Westerners celebrate the leadership of the Eastern Church. Hence we made it clear that we were confessing only the sins and errors of the Western churches. Even so, in the end, the Eastern

Orthodox members of the group refused to support the statement. Perhaps a compromise would have been possible by stating that it was individual Christians only who erred and sinned, but the Westerners felt the need to confess the errors of the Western churches in their teachings and actions, and the Easterners would not agree that churches can err. Obviously, process theologians are fully Western on this point, as on many others.

I end on this cautionary note because it would be misleading to think that in fact the community of Western process theologians and the community of Greek Orthodox theologians would share more across the board than process theologians share with the heirs of the Reformation or with contemporary Roman Catholics. Eastern Orthodoxy has great appeal today to many Protestants, but this appeal is chiefly to those who want to avoid the challenges that the modern and postmodern worlds have directed at the Western churches. Whereas process thinkers are likely to emphasize the great changes that have taken place in church and society and the need for continual rethinking and transformation, the appeal of Eastern Orthodoxy is that the church remains the same throughout the centuries. Of course, I exaggerate. No one supposes total changelessness of any institution within history, but the radically historical thinking characteristic of process theologians has its roots in the West, and Eastern thinking is, from our point of view, remarkably ahistorical.

These comments about difference are not intended to detract from the remarkable affinities. Whenever we can work together, we rejoice in doing so. But on many issues important to us, such as gender and sexuality, we will probably have to agree to differ for some time to come.

Can process thought help improve the understanding of Islam and build bridges to it?

Process theologians have been concerned about and involved in dialogue with representatives of other religious traditions for many years. Christians have been in the lead, but today members of other faith communities use process thought as a means of understanding religious diversity and approaching dialogue. David Griffin has edited a book, *Deep Religious Pluralism,* which includes Jewish, Muslim, Chinese, Buddhist, and Hindu voices of this kind.

The most distinctive contribution of Whiteheadian thought to the discussion among the religious traditions is the distinction between creativity and God, as well as noting also the kind of ultimacy attributable to the world. We can see that deep religious feeling can be attached to all three. This frees us to recognize the depth of the difference between such traditions as Buddhism and Christianity and also that they are complementary rather than in contradiction to one another. Buddhism orients us to creativity, biblical Christianity to God. In both there have been tendencies to reverence the world as well.

At the same time, this Whiteheadian vision enables us to see that some strands of Buddhism bring God into the picture. These are found especially in Pure Land Buddhism and in the Lotus Sutra. Certainly some strands of Christianity, especially mystical ones, bring creativity into the picture, often identified as "Being Itself" or the Godhead. Quite a lot has been done to sort these matters out. My book *Beyond Dialogue* contributed to this process.

Process theologians have been involved also in dialogues among the Abrahamic traditions. All of these traditions focus primarily on God, and all have mystical elements that are more oriented to the ultimate that Whitehead identified as creativity. Sorting out these distinctions contributes less to these dialogues than to dialogues with non-Abrahamic traditions.

Furthermore, process theologians are necessarily critical of the dominant and official theologies of all three of the major Abrahamic faiths. Christian process theologians devote themselves primarily to criticizing Christian traditions. Since much that they object to in Christianity is found also in Judaism and in Islam, they cannot avoid criticism of these traditions as well. This makes our role in these dialogues quite different from that in other dialogues. Our role here is to encourage some tendencies within all three traditions and to oppose others.

Even if process theology's contribution to these dialogues is less distinctive, it does come down strongly on some disputed points. Most important may be the emphatic insistence that Christians, Muslims, and Jews all worship the same God. For us, this statement is unequivocal because we make a clear distinction between that which we worship and our way of understanding what we worship. This distinction reflects our rejection of the "linguistic turn" in philosophy. We believe that language, including religious language, has a referential element. That is, when we use the word God, we refer to a reality whose exact nature and working we know that we do not know. We are open to learning more about the one God to whom we refer. We understand that our present views may change quite drastically in the process, but this does not mean that the God in whom we believe with better understanding will be a different God.

Of course, there may be a change of "gods." We may at some point recognize that what we earlier called "God" does not exist or is, in fact, an idol. We come then to speak of the true "God." This still does not mean that we understand the true God fully or adequately. Also, the problem of idolatry is found, and emphasized, in all the Abrahamic faiths.

A few years ago, *The Christian Century*, the leading Protestant ecumenical magazine, ran a series of articles on the question of whether the God of Islam and the God of Christianity are the same. Some writers seemed to think that if the nature of God is described differently in the two traditions, they worship different Gods. For those who have taken the turn to linguistic philosophy, this makes some sense. For process theologians it does not.

Process theology calls on persons of faith in all three traditions to give up their absolutes. Process theology sees no possibility of absolute knowledge or absolute authority. Everything accessible to us is creaturely. This does not exclude the presence and active participation of the Divine, but the presence of the Divine never excludes the presence of the creaturely as well. All the Abrahamic traditions possess tendencies to recognize this, but other tendencies lead toward exempting something from this general condition of conditionedness and fallibility. From the perspective of process thought, any such exemption brings in the taint of idolatry. We believe that to the extent that all three traditions can free themselves from this taint, they will be better able to live together in peace and mutual respect. As long as they absolutize what is creaturely, the best we can hope for is tolerance.

Process theology believes that all three traditions suffer from misleading doctrines about God's power. Although all three depend for the meaningfulness of much of their teaching on the view that human beings have responsibility for how they act, all three also have teachings that imply or directly affirm that God determines exactly what happens. Process theology directly challenges this belief wherever it appears and encourages understandings of God's power that are compatible with and support the understanding of human responsibility. We think the idea that God controls everything has done great harm in all three communities and has harmed also their relation to the rest of the world. We think all three traditions contain grounds to see God's power as that of empowering creatures, especially human beings, rather than as denying power to them.

This deep conviction of the need for repentance in all three communities can contribute to dialogue by removing any tendency to view one's own tradition as pure and perfect, with the problems lying only in the others. For us, as Christians, it is particularly important that we approach both Jews and Muslims in a spirit of confession. We have sinned egregiously against both. Some of what we do not like in the other communities is largely due to our crimes against them. Our faith in Jesus Christ, instead of inspiring us to humble service of our Jewish and Muslim neighbors, has led us to engage in pogroms and crusades to punish them for not sharing our beliefs. This has been a total and disastrous perversion of faith based on absolutizing a certain relation to particular, contingent historical events. Until we remove this beam from our own eyes, we are in no position to say much about the splinters in the eyes of Jews and Muslims. But those splinters do exist and badly need to be removed.

Christian process theologians can work with other Christians to overcome Christian prejudices against the Qur'an and Mohammed. We should deeply admire and appreciate the Qur'an. It is a truly remarkable document. We may object to a few of its formulations, but we have far less reason to object to the Qur'an than to much that is in our own Bible.

We do have one advantage in comparison with Islam. The Bible never claims any absolutist status for itself. Since it contradicts itself in all kinds of ways, it makes wholly clear that whatever its divine inspiration it is a thoroughly human set of writings. In other words, any open-minded approach to the Bible will quickly recognize that everything in it is historically conditioned and fallible. This is not true of the Qur'an. Its consistency and beauty of language and its claims for itself make it far harder to recognize its creaturely character. In other words, its great superiority over the Bible in many respects encourages its absolutization.

Christians are hardly in position to criticize. They have often managed to absolutize the Bible in spite of all the obstacles to doing so. However, as process theologians who strongly oppose any such absolutization of the Bible or of Jesus, we must also encourage trends within Islam to recognize that its holy book is a product of its time and place.

Christians have difficulty appreciating the greatness of Mohammed as a "prophet." This is because, for us, the prophetic tradition is that of such figures as Amos, Micah, Isaiah, and Jeremiah, a tradition that culminated in Jesus. Mohammed was a political and military leader, and in those capacities committed violent deeds. We have difficulty thinking of him as a worthy successor of Jesus. It is even harder to think of him as transcending Jesus.

If we are to appreciate the Muslim view, we must remember that among Jews there is more appreciation for Moses and David than for those associated with the prophetic books so prized by Christians. Moses and David were political and military figures who were also of great religious importance. For Jews and Muslims, those who act out their faith on the stage of history are the greatest prophets. In doing so, certainly, they engaged in violence against their enemies. But a teaching and example that can actually guide behavior on the world stage may be seen as superior to one that is applicable only in limited contexts. For this reason, despite the great reverence in which Muslims hold Jesus, Mohammed is seen as standing above or beyond him as the supreme prophet.

Christians do not need to agree with these assessments, but we should understand and respect them. After two millennia we are still confused about how to apply Jesus' message to our own lives and, far more, about its application in affairs of state. We are hardly in position to criticize Mohammed for the way he dealt with the problems that arose in these contexts. Nor should we criticize Muslims for appreciating the greater practicability of following their authorities. We should honor them also for refusing to divinize Mohammed as we have divinized Jesus.

Process theologians are sensitive to the importance of history in regard to all questions, including the role and status of traditions. We recognize that Christianity was transformed for good and for evil by the "Enlightenment" and its subordination of religious faith to nationalism. Today we are becoming keenly aware of the evil effects on us of this movement. Nevertheless, much of the hostility directed by the West against Islam is from the perspective of the Enlightenment, including its recent expressions in the sexual revolution and women's liberation. Much of the criticism would apply equally to the Christianity that antedated the Enlightenment. In contemporary Islam we can get a sense of what Christianity was like before the

Enlightenment. We can see the important values that the Enlightenment destroyed and that are still preserved in Islam. We can see also what we have gained. We can understand why Muslims are not eager to follow our lead. We can also identify changes that we hope they will make.

"No one comes to the Father except by me" (Jn. 14:6) is a stumbling block to interreligious dialogue. How do you exegete this verse? Can it be understood in a less exclusivist way?

Before I answer the question directly, indicating other ways of exegeting the text, let us recognize that the early Christian writings include an exclusivist note. The spirit of the early Christians included a strong emphasis on the new reality that Jesus, and no one else, had brought into the world. Jesus was not for them one "savior" or "lord" among others. His coming had changed the situation in which everyone lived, whether they recognized this or not.

The nature of the change is described in a variety of ways. Paul tells us that whereas prior to Jesus, the righteousness of God appeared as wrath against sin, in Jesus it appeared as love. Of course, Paul found prophesies and even anticipations of this in earlier prophets and writers, but the change occurred decisively only in Jesus. We now live by participation in his faithfulness rather than by obeying the Mosaic Law or any other law. These affirmations distinguished the communities that Paul founded from those communities that continued more traditional forms of Judaism.

Paul did not think of these as two equally valid forms of Judaism. If today we argue that the covenant with God through Christ does not supersede the covenant of the Jews with God, Paul would probably partly agree with us and partly disagree. He expected the end of history shortly, and in this end believers would share the resurrection-transformation of Jesus. However, the whole of creation, including certainly the other Jews, would also share in the final transformation. Paul's exclusivism did not condemn all who failed to join the movement, but it certainly privileged those who did.

John does not image the transformation effected by Jesus in the same way. He talks about "eternal life," which is probably equivalent to "coming to the Father." In John's view, Jesus provided a test. Some were drawn to him; others avoided him. To John, this difference was of ultimate importance. This does not mean that God punishes those who hide from the light in Jesus. Jesus came to save the whole world. Those who refuse his gifts condemn themselves to living without his gifts.

This is certainly "exclusivist." I prefer, however, a different language. For the early Christians, Jesus was a unique person who performed a unique work. For followers today to deny this because of its exclusivist character is, to me, understandable but unfortunate. I believe that the quality and character of life that Jesus made possible is unique and of great value and importance. I hope that Christians will continue to emphasize and prize this quality of life.

What is objectionable, in my view, is for those who prize one kind of life–the kind that John called "coming to the Father"–to imply that all who prize other forms of life are condemned by God, fail to achieve what they are seeking, or have no spiritual wisdom to offer. One can certainly interpret some texts in this direction, but that is to suppose that the texts were directly addressing our contemporary questions, formulated in a very different context. Today we can affirm the uniqueness of Jesus' person and of his historical work without denying the uniqueness of the person of Gautama and his historical work. That does not mean that Jesus and Gautama are two examples of one thing. They are not both incarnations of God or attainers of Buddhahood. They are profoundly different from one another. To be different does not imply that one is good and the other bad, or one important and the other unimportant. Both are both good and important.

My point in these comments is that the way ahead for Christians is to affirm the uniqueness of Jesus, the crucial importance of his work, and our discipleship to him. Precisely in being faithful, in participating in his faithfulness, we will approach other communities of wisdom and insight with open minds and open hearts, appreciating their achievements and their offering to the world. To condemn others for having found another "way" does not express participation in the faithfulness of Jesus. Often when persons who have found a rich and meaningful life in other communities encounter Jesus, they are deeply moved. Muslims hold him in very high esteem. Buddhists often suppose that he is one of the enlightened ones. Hindus often treat him as an avatar. Gandhi based much of his life work on Jesus' teaching. To suppose that Jesus would have us condemn all of these people because they have not joined Christian churches is totally unfaithful to Jesus.

John tells us that the light came into the world and that some turned away from it because their deeds were evil and they preferred darkness. Thus they condemned themselves. Gandhi did not turn away from Jesus. He followed Jesus far more closely than do the vast majority of the members of Christian churches.

If we wish to follow John closely, we should distinguish between those today who are drawn to Jesus' Sermon on the Mount and to his understanding of the *basileia theou* ("the divine commonwealth"). We would find that today the lines of division would go through the Christian communities, the Hindu communities, the Buddhist communities, and the Muslim communities. This is the light that has come into the world. Many people in all branches of the human family, including many in Christendom, prefer darkness. To say "Lord, Lord" in no way guarantees that one has actually embraced the light.

Let us note also that the main obstacle to the full appropriation of the light that shone in Jesus has been the historic behavior of Christians. When conquistadores enslaved the natives of the New World in the name of the cross of Christ, they made it hard for the natives to see in Jesus the light of which John wrote. When Christian missionaries warned Hindus that God would send them to eternal hell if they did not subscribe to Christian doctrine, they made it hard for Hindus to see this light. The response to Mother Teresa in whom the light shone, at least in some measure, was very different from the response to exclusivist anti-Hindu teachers.

I should address the original question more specifically. John's gospel is very hostile to the dominant Jewish community. Probably John's community had suffered some form of persecution at the hands of Jewish authorities. The verse in question probably reflects this hostility, expressed in so many ways in this gospel. It probably means "you Jews who rejected Jesus and reject us because of our discipleship to him have no access to the God you pretend to worship." It does not serve us well to deny that the quarrel between the followers of Jesus and those who rejected him as a false messianic claimant was sometimes a bitter one or that Jesus' followers sometimes suffered persecution from Jewish authorities. It also does not serve us well to take formulations that come out of that historical context and apply them in situations in which Jews suffer at the hands of Christian persecutors, who by their actions make it very difficult indeed for Jews to see the light that was in Jesus. We can be very grateful that when Christians have repented of their treatment of Jews, a good many Jews have come to appreciate Jesus.

Now that I have acknowledged that the original formulation probably had an exclusivist meaning over against the Jewish persecutors of Christians, I will directly discuss the question of whether another exegesis is possible. The answer is yes. This other exegesis is also closely related to the original intention of the author. His book begins by speaking of the eternal word of God. This Word functions centrally in the whole creative process. It is especially manifest in the human mind. Finally, it is fully incarnate in Jesus. Throughout John's gospel the focus is on this incarnate Word. The words that are placed on Jesus' lips in this gospel are very different from those attributed to Jesus in the synoptic gospels. In John, Jesus speaks about himself as the incarnate Word. This Word, incarnate in Jesus, is the light as well as the way, the truth, and the life. If one rejects the eternal Word, one cannot come to the Father, for they are inseparable. "The Word was with God and the Word was God. All things came into being through him" (Jn. 1:1)

The gospel of John clearly opens the door to ways of approaching the Word that do not involve Jesus. The Word that became flesh in Jesus is also found in and through all creation. No reader of the Bible as a whole can doubt that the Jewish scriptures also testify to this God who is inseparable from the Word. That Jews continue to deny the messianic claims Christians make for Jesus does not mean that they prefer darkness to light. Today some Jews and some Christians prefer the darkness. Some Jews and some Christians are drawn to the light. Unless drawn to the light, no person can come to the Father. Christians find that light uniquely embodied in Jesus. The Christian treatment of Jews has made it impossible for most Jews to see Jesus as the incarnation of the light. Those Jews who have been able to separate Jesus from Christian crimes against Jews, and who are now appropriating Jesus as an important Jewish teacher, are convinced that Christians have exaggerated Jesus' uniqueness. They emphasize the continuities between Jesus and other Jewish teachers and are teaching Christians much about these.

My point is that in general the statement that no one can come to the Father apart from the Word, or Wisdom, or Spirit of God does not exclude Jews in general, any more than Christians in general, from access to God. No doubt the author of John thought that the Jews who so strongly opposed Jesus showed thereby a blindness to the light that Jesus embodied. Perhaps this was true, at least in part. The establishment in every culture tends to be blind to reasons for its disestablishment and to take destructive actions to preserve its power. Those without vested interests in the structure of the society of Jesus' day heard Jesus gladly. That the poor and oppressed, who believed Jesus, thought that those who rejected him preferred darkness makes a good deal of sense. Their refusal of Jesus' teaching showed their priorities. Those priorities did not put God's truth first. Without doing that, they could not come to the Father.

We have learned long since that being a member of a Christian church, even a leader in the church, in no way ensures that one puts the service of God first. Enjoyment of the prerogatives of leadership all too often takes precedence. Many, many of us Christians fail the test of welcoming the light. Many of us, too, block ourselves from coming to the Father.

Both the question and my answer point to the ambiguity of canonization. On the one hand, this is an important, even essential, process for a community. By specifying the writings in relationship to which it identifies itself and establishes its norms, a community provides a shared basis for discussion of basic questions. The courts in the United States could not function without knowing the authoritative documents that determine what is legally acceptable and what should not be permitted. An academic department or guild decides what extant writings are central to its current responsibilities. Not everything can be up for grabs.

But we always face the danger that even informal canonization will give excessive authority to particular past formulations in any field. This danger is most acute when the canonization is formal and official and when the community is a religious one. Our Christian canon is profoundly inspiring and life giving, but it is full of mistakes of all kinds—historical, ethical, and religious. Some of the worst of these are in the gospel of John, and they are especially about Jews. When Christianity was a politically and religiously powerless and persecuted movement, its lashing out against its enemies, while not admirable, was certainly understandable. When this lashing out is canonized, the tendency is to dehistoricize it—that is, to suppose that judgments about particular people at a particular time have universal truth. For two centuries, Christian scholars have been studying the canon in much the way they would study any ancient writings. This, too, is ambiguous in its consequences, but it has liberated those who attend to it from the dehistoricized approach to the canon. Sadly, most preaching, and even most Bible study, deals only tangentially with this scholarship or ignores it altogether. Accordingly, people in the pew are left with the supposition that as Christians, they *should* believe things that in the current situation can only prove harmful.

Perhaps a simple rule of thumb might be this. Begin with the summary of the law: Love God and neighbor. Do not believe anything that reduces this love or leads to action that fails to express it.

Bibliography

Bernanos, Georges. *Diary of a Country Priest*. 1936. New York: Carroll & Graf, 1984.

Bracken, Joseph P., S.J., and Marjorie Hewitt Suchocki. *Trinity in Process*. New York: Continuum, 2005.

Bohm, David, and Basil J. Hiley. *The Undivided Universe: An Ontological Interpretation of Quantum Theory*. London: Routledge, 1993.

Christ, Carol P. *She Who Changes*. New York: Palgrave Macmillan, 2003.

Cobb, John B. Jr. *Beyond Dialogue*. 1982. Eugene, Ore.: Wipf & Stock, 1998.

———. *Christ in a Pluralistic Age*. 1975. Eugene, Ore.: Wipf & Stock, 1998.

———. *A Christian Natural Theology*. 2d ed. Louisville: Westminster John Knox, 2007.

———. *Is It Too Late? A Theology of Ecology*. Beverly Hills, Calif.: Bruce, 1972.

Cobb, John B., Jr., and Herman E. Daly. *For the Common Good*. 1989. Boston: Beacon Press, 1994.

Cobb, John B., Jr., and David Lull. *Romans*. Chalice Commentary Series for Today. St. Louis: Chalice Press, 2005.

Dorrien, Gary. *The Making of American Liberal Theology: Crisis, Irony, & Postmodernity, 1950–2005*. Louisville: Westminster John Knox Press, 2006.

Fitzgerald, Michael. "Physicist and Priest: An Interview with John Polkinghorne," *The Christian Century*, January 29, 2008.

Griffin, David Ray, ed. *Deep Religious Pluralism*. Louisville: Westminster John Knox Press, 2005.

———. *Parapyschology, Philosophy, and Spirituality: A Postmodern Exploration*. Albany: State University of New York Press, 1997.

Hartshorne, Charles. *Born to Sing*. Bloomington: Indiana University Press, 1973.

——. *The Philosophy and Psychology of Sensation.* Chicago: University of Chicago Press, 1934.

Lewis, C. S. *The Great Divorce.* 1945. San Francisco: HarperOne, 2001.

Lovelock, James. *The Revenge of Gaia: Earth's Climate Crisis and the Fate of Humanity.* New York: Basic Books, 2006.

Meadows, Donella, Jorgen Randers, and Dennis Meadows. *The Limits to Growth.* New York: Universe Books, 1972.

Placher, Willam C. "Liberal Heroes." *The Christian Century,* May 7, 2009.

Pothen, George. "Relational Cosmologies of Gregory of Nyssa and Alfred North Whitehead." PhD diss., Claremont Graduate University, 2000.

Process & Faith Web site. http://www.processandfaith.org.

Schwartz, Peter, and Doug Randall. *An Abrupt Climate Change Scenario and Its Implications for United States National Security.* http://www.edf.org/documents/3566_AbruptClimateChange.pdf. Accessed September 20, 2010.

Suchocki, Marjorie Hewitt. *The End of Evil.* 1988. Eugene, Ore.: Wipf & Stock, 2005.

Whitehead, Alfred North. *Process and Reality.* 1927. Corrected Edition. Edited by David Ray Griffin and Donald W. Sherburne. New York: Free Press, 1978.

——. *Religion in the Making.* 1926. New York: Fordham University Press, 1996.

——. *Science and the Modern World.* 1925. New York: Free Press, 1967.